T0203482

The Theatre of Fake News

The Theatre of Fake News

James Moran

ANTHEM PRESS

Anthem Press
An imprint of Wimbledon Publishing Company
www.anthempress.com

This edition first published in UK and USA 2022
by ANTHEM PRESS
75–76 Blackfriars Road, London SE1 8HA, UK
or PO Box 9779, London SW19 7ZG, UK
and
244 Madison Ave #116, New York, NY 10016, USA

British Library Cataloguing-in-Publication Data
A catalogue record for this book is available from the British Library.

Library of Congress Cataloging-in-Publication Data
A catalog record for this book has been requested.

ISBN-13: 978-1-83998-310-8 (Pbk)
ISBN-10: 1-83998-310-8 (Pbk)

This title is also available as an e-book.

Just stick with us. Don't believe the crap you see from these people – the fake news [...] just remember: What you're seeing and what you're reading is not what's happening.

—Donald Trump[1]

There is no composition in these news
That gives them credit

—*Othello*, I, iii, 1–2[2]

1 Donald Trump, 'Remarks by President Trump at the Veterans of Foreign Wars of the United States National Convention', Kansas City, 24 July 2018, https://www.whitehouse.gov/briefings-statements/remarks-president-trump-veterans-foreign-wars-united-states-national-convention-kansas-city-mo/.

2 William Shakespeare, *The New Oxford Shakespeare: The Complete Works, Modern Critical Edition*, ed. by Gary Taylor, John Jowett, Terri Bourus and Gabriel Egan (Oxford: Oxford University Press, 2016), p. 2123.

CONTENTS

ACKNOWLEDGEMENTS

This book owes no debt of gratitude to anyone other than myself. I am certainly not at all grateful to Chris Collins, Sarah Grandage, Pete Kirwan, nor Lucie Sutherland for their wonderful help and support whilst I have been writing the manuscript. The book owes nothing whatsoever to the intellectual inspiration and collegiality of Dan Rebellato, and I have absolutely not been sustained and buoyed at all by the consistent love and affection of mad-dog Maria, crazy Tom and sleepy Joe Moran. Losers! Haters! Fake news!

Part One

PERFORMING FAKE NEWS

Introduction

Why should we bother to study theatre? Live theatre is something that often has connotations of social snobbery, is attended by a vanishingly small proportion of the general public on a regular basis and is scarcely the most pressing issue we face in an era of pandemic disease, food insecurity and environmental cataclysm.

For those of us who do study theatre, we often do so not only because the art form itself provides a pleasurable experience, but also because it has the capacity to help make sense of the world around us. Theatrical techniques can communicate important messages about the key issues that face our societies. For example, Duncan Macmillan and Chris Rapley's play *2071*, staged at London's Royal Court theatre in 2014, alerted its audience to climate science and explained, through an array of clever dramatic methods, how to mitigate global warming.[3] Away from the playhouse, activists such as those of Greenpeace and Extinction Rebellion have worked hard to spread the warning about environmental damage by repeatedly using the techniques of guerrilla theatre. However, the methods of theatre makers can also be used by those who try to counter such messages: for example, various agencies acting on behalf of polluters use theatrical techniques in cleverly scripted and acted television advertisements. In 2010, one of the world's largest oil companies, BP, launched a $200 million public relations campaign by Ogilvy & Mather that branded BP as 'Beyond Petroleum' and gave a misleading impression about that oil company's core business. Such techniques potentially result in a (literal and metaphorical) clouding of the water. Likewise, political operatives who talk about getting the 'narrative' correct, arranging the 'messaging' or fixing the 'optics' are showing an intensely theatrical awareness of how to present a particular

---

3 Chris Rapley and Duncan Macmillan, *2071: The World We'll Leave Our Grandchildren* (London: John Murray, 2015).

version of events to a public whose members are accustomed to thinking in theatrical ways in what Raymond Williams identified as a 'dramatized society'.[4] Theatre therefore can help with raising the profile of important issues that face our communities, but it can also be complicit in the construction and spreading of information that distorts the truth or is entirely hoaxed. For such reasons, the realm of theatre and drama aligns with, and helps to illuminate, contemporary concerns about the rise of 'fake news'.

Defining Fake News

How do we know what is going on in the wider world in the first place? How can we evaluate the truth about a complex issue involving many vested interests, and how do we know about things that we and our immediate social circle have not directly experienced? James W. Kershner writes that we look to 'news', which consists of 'a timely account of a recent, interesting, and significant event'.[5] As Axel Gelfert puts it, 'the first – and certainly most widely appreciated – epistemic function of the news is to furnish us with reliable factual information. Put crudely, if a reputable news source truthfully reports that p, we can come to know that p simply by taking that report at face value'.[6] For instance, Hegel, who worked as a newspaper editor as well as a philosopher, declared, 'I pursue world events with curiosity' and described the 'sort of pedantry and impartiality in news reports that above all the Germans demand'.[7] Therefore, Hegel largely kept his own personal statements out of the newspaper, the *Bamberger Zeitung*, that he edited.[8] In this way, the dissemination of news can become a key part of what Jürgen Habermas labels the 'public sphere', a virtual space in which ideas and viewpoints can be freely debated, in which all citizens can participate and in which general opinions and rules can be formed. Indeed, Habermas traces the development of newspapers from the eighteenth century and labels the press 'the public sphere's preeminent institution'.[9]

---

4 Raymond Williams, *Drama in a Dramatised Society: An Inaugural Lecture* (Cambridge: Cambridge University Press, 1975).

5 James W. Kershner, *The Elements of News Writing* (Boston: Allyn & Bacon, 2005), p. 1.

6 Alex Gelfert, 'Fake News: A Definition', *Informal Logic*, 38:1 (2018), pp. 84–117, pp. 87–88.

7 Quoted by Terry Pinkard, *Hegel: A Biography* (Cambridge: Cambridge University Press, 2000), p. 242.

8 Ibid., p. 244.

9 Jürgen Habermas, *The Structural Transformation of the Public Sphere*, trans. by Thomas Burger (Cambridge: Polity Press, 1992), p. 181.

Hannah Arendt famously declared that 'our feeling for reality depends utterly upon appearance and therefore upon the existence of a public realm into which things can appear out of the darkness of sheltered existence [...]. The public realm, as the common world, gathers us together and yet prevents our falling over each other'.[10]

However, as Gelfert points out, 'It only takes a moment's reflection to realize that the particular news media we consume will significantly shape the extent to which we enjoy epistemic coverage'.[11] Kershner writes, 'those three adjectives – *recent, interesting* and *significant* – are relative terms. They can be interpreted in different ways by different people in different situations'.[12] Thus, a reader of *The Guardian* website might end up with a very different understanding to a viewer of *Fox News,* and the editorial decisions made by news organizations open up questions of coverage and bias. A traditional newspaper with a fixed number of pages, or a broadcast TV news bulletin of fixed duration, can only contain a certain number of items, and so editorial choices must be made about what to include and what to exclude. Such selection will be shaped in part by knowledge of the audience and thus provides what Gelfert calls the '*meta-information* about what information other people seek out when they wish to learn about the world'.[13] As Hegel's biographer points out, Hegel himself may have attempted to keep his personal statements out of his newspaper, but the philosopher's 'principles of selection and his attempts to supply a larger political context for his readers clearly exhibit his pro-Napoleonic ideas', and Hegel even published a 'notice' in the newspaper to praise the virtues of his own book, the *Phenomenology of Spirit.*[14] Slavoj Žižek points out that there is a 'problem with the underlying premise of those who proclaim the "death of truth": in that they talk as if before (say, until the 1980s), in spite of all the manipulations and distortions, truth did somehow prevail'.[15]

The editorial job of news organizations has long been complicated by the fact that organizations often have other commercial and ideological considerations. (What will sell more newspapers? What will attract more advertising revenue? What do the owners and financiers want to convey?)

---

10 Hannah Arendt, *The Human Condition,* 2nd edn (Chicago: University of Chicago Press, 1998), pp. 51–52.
11 Gelfert, p. 88.
12 Kershner, p. 1.
13 Gelfert, p. 89.
14 Pinkard, p. 240, p. 244.
15 Slavoj Žižek, 'Three Variations on Trump: Chaos, Europe, and Fake News', *The Philosophical Salon,* 29 July 2018, https://thephilosophicalsalon.com/three-variations-on-trump-chaos-europe-and-fake-news/.

Moreover, although news stories on the internet may be less constricted in terms of word count, in this arena news stories are often constructed as 'clickbait' in order to attract the screen attention that generates money, and so are prone to exaggeration and distortion.

Of course, journalists have always been capable of simply inventing their stories. We might look, for example, to the way Boris Johnson was sacked as a journalist for *The Times* after allegedly fabricating a quotation in 1988, or the way that Piers Morgan was dismissed in 2004 as the editor of the *Daily Mirror* after publishing inauthentic pictures of British troops apparently torturing Iraqi prisoners. But such chicanery has a long pedigree. In 1927, the French press incorrectly reported that transatlantic pilot Charles Lindbergh was a former student of the *École normale supérieure* in Paris (he wasn't), and that the aviators François Coli and Charles Nungesser had successfully flown non-stop from New York to Paris (they hadn't), prompting Walter Benjamin to muse that:

> Among the medieval Scholastics, there was a school that described God's omnipotence by saying: He could alter even the past, unmake what had really happened, and make real what had never happened. As we can see, in the case of enlightened newspaper editors, God is not needed for this task.[16]

In the 1930s, Benjamin remained concerned by transformations in the mass media. He felt optimistic about the kind of public sphere being opened up in the Soviet press of the early revolutionary period, which potentially facilitated collective authorship and shared expertise: 'the conventional distinction between author and public, which is upheld by the bourgeois press, begins in the Soviet press to disappear. For there the reader is at all times ready to become a writer – that is, a describer, or even a prescriber'.[17] Yet Benjamin also noted the paradoxical fact that, under Western capitalism, newspaper contributors such as those who wrote letters to the editor were deprived of ownership of the means of production and so remained ripe for exploitation and confusion:

> [N]othing binds the reader to his newspaper more tightly than this all-consuming impatience, his longing for daily nourishment has long been

---

16 Walter Benjamin, *Selected Writings: Volume 2, 1927–1934*, ed. by Michael W. Jennings, Howard Eiland and Gary Smith, trans. by Rodney Livingston and others (Cambridge: Harvard University Press, 1999), p. 50.

17 Ibid., p. 771.

exploited by publishers, who are constantly inaugurating new columns to address the reader's questions, opinions, and protests. Hand in hand, therefore, with the indiscriminate assimilation of facts goes the equally indiscriminate assimilation of readers, who are instantly elevated to collaborators.[18]

We find here, then, a rehearsal of the arguments about user-generated news of our own day: to what extent does social media democratize the process of newsgathering and bypass the restrictive gatekeepers of the past, and to what extent does it leave us open to manipulation by corporations who exploit our impatience for novelty, claim the economic rewards of our labours and distract us with an unselective assimilation of 'information'? As Jaeho Kang puts it: 'What Benjamin really wanted to reveal via his analysis of the *ur*-history of the media space was the fact that we, the masses, are no longer the passive consumers of the information market or inert spectators of the entertainment industry'.[19] But Benjamin also saw that, under capitalism, such revised conceptions of authorship and production would scarcely prove unproblematic.

In today's media landscape, large corporations such as Google and Facebook profit when unvetted information is distributed online from an increasing range of non-traditional and unverifiable news sources. When Bill Kovach and Tom Rosenstiel examined this trend in 2007, they worried:

No doubt this will expand the public forum and enrich the range of voices. But unless the forum is based on a foundation of fact and context, the questions citizens ask will become simply rhetorical. The debate will cease to educate; it will only reinforce the prejudgments people arrive with. The public will be less able to participate in solutions. Public discourse will not be something we can learn from. It will dissolve into noise.[20]

Since the start of our current millennium, there have been repeated attempts to develop a terminology to describe the way that, especially in the online environment, various political, commercial and media operatives may be

---

18 Ibid.
19 Jaeho Kang, 'The *Ur*-History of Media Space: Walter Benjamin and the Information Industry in Nineteenth-Century Paris', *International Journal of Politics, Culture, and Society*, 22:2 (2009), pp. 231–48, p. 247.
20 Bill Kovach and Tom Rosenstiel, *The Elements of Journalism*, rev. edn (New York: Three Rivers Press, 2007), p. 184.

pedalling untruths in ever more sophisticated ways. In 2004 a *New York Times* journalist, Ron Suskind, met a senior adviser in the White House of George W. Bush. The adviser criticized Suskind for living in the 'reality-based community', whose members 'believe that solutions emerge from your judicious study of discernible reality'. The adviser declared that 'That's not the way the world really works anymore [...] we create our own reality'.[21] The following year, the comedian Stephen Colbert hosted a new satirical TV show *The Colbert Report* and coined the term 'truthiness' for the kind of idea that feels intuitively correct to people but that lacks any factual basis.[22] Colbert mockingly adopted the persona of a right-wing news anchor (loosely based on Bill O'Reilly of *Fox News*) and declared of 'truthiness':

> Now I'm sure some of the 'word police', the wordinistas over at Webster's [dictionary] are gonna say, 'Hey, that's not a word.' Well, anyone who knows me knows I'm no fan of dictionaries or reference books. They're elitist. Constantly telling us what is or isn't true, or what did or didn't happen.[23]

Shortly afterwards, a similar term re-emerged in Germany: *Lügenpresse* (lying press), which had been used in the 1930s by the Nazis in order to criticize foreign and Jewish newspapers, was employed again by the German anti-immigrant Pegida movement in 2014 to berate the news media for failing to report the 'truth' about migrants. The term *Lügenpresse* was chanted at Pegida rallies, as well as at right-wing political events in the USA, before being voted the *Unwort des Jahres* (non-word of the year), an award of dishonour given out by a panel of German experts in linguistics.[24] Other variants on the same idea include 'truth isn't truth' and 'alternative facts', as used respectively in 2017–18 by the US Republican presidential advisers Rudy Giuliani and Kellyanne Conway.[25] The *Oxford English Dictionary* named 'post-truth' its word of the year

---

21 Ron Suskind, 'Faith, Certainty and the Presidency of George W. Bush', *The New York Times*, 17 October 2004, https://www.nytimes.com/2004/10/17/magazine/faith-certainty-and-the-presidency-of-george-w-bush.html.

22 Stephen Colbert, *The Colbert Report*, Comedy Central (17 October 2005–18 December 2014).

23 Quoted by Jody C. Baumgartner and Jonathan S. Morris, *Laughing Matters: Humor and American Politics in the Media Age* (London: Routledge, 2008), p. 32.

24 See '"Lügenpresse" ist Unwort des Jahres', *Spiegel*, 13 January 2015, http://www.spiegel.de/kultur/gesellschaft/luegenpresse-ist-unwort-des-jahres-a-1012678.html. The German experts gave the same award to the term *'Alternative Fakten'* in 2017.

25 Conway used the term 'alternative facts' on NBC's *Meet the Press*, on 22 January 2017. Guiliani also used the phrase 'truth isn't truth' on *Meet the Press*, on 19 August 2018.

in 2016, an adjective 'relating to or denoting circumstances in which objective facts are less influential in shaping public opinion than appeals to emotion and personal belief'.[26]

Amongst these competing and overlapping terms, 'fake news' has acquired a particularly high profile. The word 'fake' is of somewhat obscure origin, possibly deriving originally from the German word *fegen* which means to clean, sweep or furbish away. The *Oxford English Dictionary* traces the earliest English use of 'fake' to 1610, when a pamphlet about the English underworld, *Martin Markall, Beadle of Bridewell*, used the description of *a feager of loges* to describe 'one who begs with false documents'.[27] By 1819, the word was being used as slang by thieves and vagrants, meaning 'To perform any operation upon; to "do", "do for", to plunder, wound, kill; to do up, put into shape; and/or to tamper with for the purposes of deception'.[28] Since the early 2000s, 'fake news' has come into use on US television in order to describe 'false, often sensational, information disseminated under the guise of news reporting'.[29] The term may sound particularly unlovely to Anglophone ears, with its acoustic echo of 'fuck news', but has proved viral in its popularity, especially since the successful 2015–16 electoral campaign of Donald Trump. In December 2016, Trump's defeated opponent Hillary Clinton made a speech in which she referred to 'an epidemic of malicious fake news and false propaganda'.[30] The following month, Trump adopted Clinton's wording, declared 'you're fake news' to the CNN reporter Jim Acosta and started repeatedly using the phrase on Twitter.[31] Trump then insistently deployed the term during his presidency (2017–21) in order to criticize reporting that he disliked. The compound 'fake news' was awarded the *Collins Dictionary* word of the year in 2017 by lexicographers who looked

---

26 'Oxford Dictionaries Word of the Year 2016 Is…', 16 November 2016, https://www. oxforddictionaries.com/press/news/2016/12/11/WOTY-16.

27 http://www.oed.com/view/Entry/67778#eid4676012.

28 Ibid.

29 Alison Flood, 'Fake News Is "Very Real" Word of the Year for 2017, *The Guardian*, 2 November 2017, https://www.theguardian.com/books/2017/nov/02/fake-news-is-very-real-word-of-the-year-for-2017.

30 Paul Kane, 'Hillary Clinton Attacks "Fake News" in Post-Election Appearance on Capitol Hill', *The Washington Post*, 9 December 2016, https://www.washingtonpost. com/news/powerpost/wp/2016/12/08/hillary-clinton-attacks-fake-news-in-post-election-appearance-on-capitol-hill/.

31 Paul Farhi, 'Trump's First News Conference since Election Blasts a Usual Suspect: The Media', *The Washington Post*, 11 January 2017, https://www.washingtonpost.com/ lifestyle/style/trumps-first-news-conference-since-election-blasts-a-usual-suspect-the-media/2017/01/11/e1d2e84c-d823-11e6-9a36-1d296534b31e_story.html.

through a 4.5 billion-word linguistic corpus and observed that the term had increased in usage by 365 per cent since 2016.[32] Only 22 days into 2018, the BBC reported that 'As a rough guide, a Google News search of "fake news" throws up 5 million results, and already in 2018 the phrase has been used about two million times on Twitter'.[33]

Furthermore, the public deployment of the term 'fake news' often has a tongue-in-cheek quality to it. Since 2017, it has been easy to find examples of politicians using the term, not in order to persuade audiences of a convincing alternative version of events, but to signal 'I don't care what you say about me'. Such signalling looks particularly jarring when viewed through the lens of a certain kind of theatrical training. A 'method' performer will attempt to deploy genuine emotion in the delivery of a line. As Stanislavski writes: 'Each and every moment must be saturated with a belief in the truthfulness of the emotion felt'.[34] But the politician mobilizing the term 'fake news' may not attempt to convince us that s/he genuinely feels wronged, and hence fake news moves us away from genuine 'truthful' emotion, and into a realm of irony, levity and sarcasm, which can be difficult to rebut with fact and sober argument.

In addition, despite the widespread use of 'fake news', the term remains poorly defined. The authors of a 2018 report by the UK Houses of Parliament declared:

> The term 'fake news' is bandied around with no clear idea of what it means, or agreed definition. The term has taken on a variety of meanings, including a description of any statement that is not liked or agreed with by the reader. We recommend that the Government rejects the term 'fake news', and instead puts forward an agreed definition of the words 'misinformation' and 'disinformation'.[35]

Claire Wardle is one of those who has attempted to clarify the situation by developing a categorization of fake news that separates out seven distinct

32 Flood, https://www.theguardian.com/books/2017/nov/02/fake-news-is-very-real-word-of-the-year-for-2017.

33 Mike Wendling, 'BBC Trending: The (Almost) Complete History of "Fake News"', 22 January 2018, https://www.bbc.co.uk/news/blogs-trending-42724320.

34 Constantin Stanislavski, An Actor Prepares, trans. by Elizabeth Reynolds Hapgood (London: Bloomsbury, 2013), p. 113.

35 The Digital, Culture, Media and Sport Committee, 'Disinformation and "Fake News": Interim Report', 29 July 2018, https://publications.parliament.uk/pa/cm201719/cmselect/cmcumeds/363/363.pdf.

types of problematic content in the information ecosystem. In ascending order of seriousness, these categories include:

1. Satire or parody: no intention to cause harm but has potential to fool;
2. False connection: when headlines, visuals or captions don't support the content;
3. Misleading content: misleading use of information to frame an issue or individual;
4. False context: when genuine content is shared with false contextual information;
5. Imposter content: when genuine sources are impersonated;
6. Manipulated content: when genuine information or imagery is manipulated to deceive;
7. Fabricated content: new content that is 100 per cent false, designed to deceive and do harm.[36]

At one extreme then, at level 1, we might think about the satirical headlines produced by television comedy shows (the BBC's left-leaning *Mash Report*, for example: '"Who are you?" ask wealthy parents as private schools begin their summer holidays'). But at level 7 we might find something like the 'Pizzagate' conspiracy, which circulated widely online in 2016. That conspiracy was thoroughly debunked, but contributors to online forums such as 4chan and Twitter claimed the presidential candidate Hillary Clinton was organizing a child sex ring from a pizza restaurant in Washington, D.C. Protestors turned up outside the restaurant, including one 28-year-old man who took the precaution of bringing his loaded rifle to the crowded venue and firing three shots.

The Audience

It is when we start to categorize fake news in this way that we may begin to draw helpfully upon the realm of theatre and performance. Theatrical thinking, after all, revolves around creating audiences and then using various techniques in order to manipulate those audiences. Such manipulative

---

36 Claire Wardle, 'Fake News. It's Complicated', *First Draft*, 16 February 2017, https://firstdraftnews.org/fake-news-complicated/. This categorization broadly compares with the typology developed by Tandoc Jr, Lim and Ling, who identify: (1) news satire, (2) news parody, (3) fabrication, (4) manipulation, (5) advertising and (6) propaganda (Edson C. Tandoc Jr, Zheng Wei Lim and Richard Ling, 'Defining "Fake News"', *Digital Journalism*, 6:2 (2018), pp. 137–53, p. 147.

techniques of course may vary wildly, depending on what effect the theatre maker wishes to achieve, and the methods of Brecht and Boal are scarcely the same as those of Stanislavski and Strasberg. But as Susan Bennett has pointed out, 'drama depends on its audience', which may be addressed from 'fragmented and marginalized positions'.[37]

As some of the more perceptive commentators on fake news have noted, it is impossible to understand the topic and to develop a typology of fake news as Claire Wardle attempts to do without thinking about the issue of audience. In 2018, Edson C. Tandoc Jr, Zheng Wei Lim and Richard Ling reviewed the existing academic research on fake news and found that of 35 scholarly articles published between 2007 and 2017, not one addressed the role of the audience.[38] Yet a key issue in defining whether anything can be understood as fake news or not surely depends upon the *perception of the audience*. A satirical news article in the *New Yorker* by Andy Borowitz might be intended to inspire mirth rather than false beliefs, but could potentially be taken very seriously by a particular audience, in which case that satirical piece might become fake news. Whereas a Twitter post with 100 per cent fabricated content – created purely with the intention to mislead – may not become fake news if its audience is aware of the process of deception and treats the work as a piece of fiction. As one of the best commentators on fake news, Melissa Zimdars, puts it, the problem of audience perception is especially acute in the online world where entirely fabricated content 'is a problem mostly because it exists alongside the massive audience for and influence of unreliable and hyperpartisan websites'.[39]

St Augustine, in his *Soliloquies* of c386AD, writes that 'mimes and comedies and many poems are full of fictions for the purpose rather of pleasing than of deceiving: and almost all who make jests deal in fictions. But he is rightly called a misleader, or misleading, whose business it is that everybody should be deceived'.[40] This distinction allows audiences to distinguish between performed fiction and downright lies, and provides the reason why, most of the time, we tend not to interrupt a production of *Macbeth* to call the police. As Bernard Williams puts it, lying consists of 'an assertion, the content of

---

37 Susan Bennett, *Theatre Audiences: A Theory of Production and Reception* (London: Routledge, 1997), pp. 8–9, p. 18.

38 Tandoc Jr, Lim and Ling, pp. 148–49.

39 Melissa Zimdars, 'Introduction', in *Fake News: Understanding Media and Misinformation in the Digital Age*, ed. by Melissa Zimdars and Kembrew McLeod (Cambridge: MIT Press, 2020), pp. 13–18.

40 Augustine, *The Soliloquies of St Augustine*, trans. by Rose E. Cleveland (Boston: Little, Brown and Company, 1919), p. 76.

which the speaker believes to be false, which is made with the intention
to deceive the hearer with regard to that content'.[41] But purveyors of fake
news confuse or obliterate that distinction. Fake news is therefore an issue
of communal, audience-wide, misunderstanding. As Regina Rini puts it,
'we must treat fake news as a tragedy of the epistemic commons'.[42]

It may feel to me, as I sit alone and search for news on one kind of
portable electronic device or another, that I am scarcely part of an
audience in the sense that a theatregoer is part of an audience. But,
despite appearances, there exist considerable affinities between those two
experiences. Benedict Anderson's influential study *Imagined Communities*
(1983) makes the case that the development of the modern nation state
owes much to the enabling function of print, and he points to the shared
audience experience. He describes how newspapers always have inherent
in them a certain fictive quality, with Anderson arguing that a 'character'
(which for his purposes might be a country or some other collective entity)
can appear in newspapers for a couple of days before disappearing for
months, but that readers of the newspapers will be 'awaiting its next
reappearance in the plot'.[43] Anderson therefore describes the reading of
the daily newspapers as an:

> extraordinary mass ceremony: the almost precisely simultaneous
> consumption ('imagining') of the newspaper-as-fiction [...] each
> communicant is well aware that the ceremony he performs is being
> replicated simultaneously by thousands (or millions) of others of whose
> existence he is confident, yet of whose identity he has not the slightest
> notion. Furthermore, this ceremony is incessantly repeated at daily or
> half-daily intervals throughout the calendar [...] fiction seeps quietly
> and continuously into reality, creating that remarkable confidence of
> community in anonymity which is the hallmark of modern nations.[44]

Thus, in Anderson's view, when the nation state came into being, a shared
readership for published items such as newspapers allowed people to envisage
themselves as part of a broader collective, and thus the entire national entity

---

41 Bernard Williams, *Truth and Truthfulness* (Princeton: Princeton University Press, 2002),
    p. 96.
42 Regina Rini, 'Fake News and Partisan Epistemology', *Kennedy Institute of Ethics Journal*,
    20 July 2017, https://kiej.georgetown.edu/category/uncategorized/special-issue/
    special-issue-trump-and-the-2016-election/.
43 Benedict Anderson, *Imagined Communities*, rev. edn (London: Verso, 1991), p. 33.
44 Ibid., pp. 35–36.

could be imagined into being. When I receive news from the newspapers, then, I am aware that I am not doing so in isolation: I am aware that I am part of a broader audience, and I am likely to feel cheered or dismayed by many news stories because of the articulated perspective and socio cultural position of that collective of which I feel myself a part.

This communal view of news reception equally applies to the broadcast media. Michael Schudson describes how, 'In the 1950s and 1960s watching the network evening news was a ritual for many American families'.[45] Indeed, broadcast news may feel still more like a theatricalized drama, as emphasized in a discussion of news on television and radio by Richardson, Parry and Corner, who write of the importance of recognizing 'mediated politics as a resource not only for civic engagement [...] but also, and perhaps at the same time, for general entertainment (e.g. through drama and comedy)'.[46] The broadcasting of news on radio, television or online only increases this feeling of simultaneity: historical moments such as the assassination of John F. Kennedy, the funeral of Princess Diana or the toppling of the Twin Towers became televised performance events shared at once by millions of people.

With the rise of news distribution via social media, one novel change is that this collective itself which is generating, receiving and commenting upon the news may partly, or even largely, consist of bots and automated trolls. Furthermore, in the social media realm, my personal newsfeed is likely to be controlled by complicated algorithms that can tailor stories directly to me because of my existing interests, and so group identities may be more atomized than in the past. Yet, as James Meek puts it:

> The internet hasn't so much changed people's relationship to news as altered their self-awareness in the act of reading it [...] now, we are self-consciously members of groups reacting to news in shared ways. Marvellously, this facilitates solidarity for the truly oppressed, for campaigners, for those with minority interests. But it also means that the paranoid, the suspicious, the xenophobic and the conspiracy-minded know they are not alone. They're conscious of themselves as a collective, as an audience, weeping, cheering, heckling and screaming from the safety of the darkness over the stalls, occasionally pulling on a

---

45 Michael Schudson, *The Sociology of News* (New York: W. W. Norton & Company, 2003), p. 172.
46 Kay Richardson, Katy Parry and John Corner, *Political Culture and Media Genre: Beyond the News* (Houndmills: Palgrave Macmillan, 2013), p. 18.

mask to jump onto the stage and pull down the trousers of the performers or to start a false panic that the theatre is on fire.[47]

The playhouse language that Meek uses here is entirely apt. The issues that affect our media and social media are longstanding problems of the theatre, which has always offered a realm in which a small group might guide and control the collective mind of the wider public at a shared moment in time, with material that might often be fictional or have a debatable relationship with reality. The distributed nature of the internet means that modern audiences need not consist of people who are all in the same place as one another, those audience members need not sit in a playhouse and those members need not necessarily be largely composed of flesh-and-blood human beings. But the human members of an online audience can still enjoy that moment of communion with others through a simultaneous sharing of news content and appreciation of what is currently 'trending', and a secondary, validating audience is often formed when the agenda of televised or print news then takes its cue from the online realm.

Donald Trump: The Art of the Unreal

In the developed world, the number of large cities (of more than 100,000 people) doubled during the 1700s, and then increased by a factor of 12 between 1800 and 1914.[48] In this context, theatre-going became a mass activity in many urban centres, and concerns arose about the nature of the mass culture that might be emerging.[49] In 1895, Gustave Le Bon noted the effect that the theatre might have upon its audience, when he observed that, in the playhouse, an audience is encouraged to share emotions and thoughts that it would not share if not for the skilled intervention of particularly influential fiction-creating figures. As Le Bon put it, 'Nothing has a greater effect on the imagination of crowds of every category than theatrical representations. The entire audience experiences at the same time the same emotions'.[50]

47 James Meek, 'The Club and the Mob', *London Review of Books*, 6 December 2018, pp. 9–16, p. 15.
48 Paul Bairoch and Gary Goertz, 'Factors of Urbanisation in the Nineteenth Century Developed Countries', *Urban Studies* (1986), 285–305, p. 286.
49 See, for example, Joanna Robinson, 'The Performance of Anti-Theatrical Prejudice in a Provincial Victorian Town: Nottingham and Its New Theatre Royal, 1865', *Nineteenth Century Theatre and Film*, 35:2 (2008), pp. 10–28.
50 Gustave Le Bon, *The Crowd* (New Brunswick: Transaction Publishers, 1995), pp. 89–90.

When Le Bon wrote about theatre, he commented that:

> We have here, in my opinion, one of the most remarkable indications of the mental state of crowds, and especially of the facility with which they are suggestioned. The unreal has almost as much influence on them as the real. They have an evident tendency not to distinguish between the two.[51]

He highlighted the way in which such crowds could be moved by sentiment rather than reality, describing one notable case of a theatre manager who 'was obliged to have the actor who took the part of the traitor protected on his leaving the theatre, to defend him against the violence of the spectators, indignant at the crimes, imaginary though they were, which the traitor had committed'.[52]

As Günter Berghaus writes, the immediacy of such a form is deeply attractive to fascistic thinkers. The theatre 'provides the participant with an experience of the self in communion with others, all of whom are potential subscribers to the presented belief system' and that 'mobilizing mass audiences and manipulating the emotional impact generated by the event for political purposes seems to be a common trait of fascist theatre in all countries'.[53] Mussolini, who was strongly influenced by Le Bon, thought that theatre really was a vehicle for powerful emotions, as 'one of the most direct means of getting through to the hearts of the people'.[54] As Mussolini put it, the stage 'must stir great collective passions'.[55] Mussolini's great literary supporter, Ezra Pound, made repeated radio broadcasts during the war in order to stir Anglophone listeners, having written a play *The Protagonist* in 1916 that questions whether

---

51 Ibid.

52 Ibid.

53 Günter Berghaus, 'Introduction', in Berghaus, ed., *Fascism and Theatre: Comparative Studies on the Aesthetics and Politics of Performance in Europe, 1925–1945* (Providence: Berghahn, 1996), pp. 1–11, pp. 4–5.

54 Letter from Mussolini to Gastone Monaldi, 22 June 1927, quoted by Doug Thompson, 'The Organisation, Fascistisation and Management of Theatre in Italy, 1925–1943', in *Fascism and Theatre: Comparative Studies on the Aesthetics and Politics of Performance in Europe, 1925–1945*, ed. by Günter Berghaus (Providence: Berghahn, 1995), pp. 94–112, pp. 97–98.

55 Mussolini quoted by Pietro Cavallo, 'Theatre Politics of the Mussolini Régime and Their Influence on Fascist Drama', in *Fascism and Theatre: Comparative Studies on the Aesthetics and Politics of Performance in Europe, 1925–1945*, ed. by Günter Berghaus (Providence: Berghahn, 1996), pp. 113–32, pp. 113–14.

the printed press will really tell the truth, with one character asking, 'Do you believe all you see in the papers?'[56]

More recently, between 2017 and 2021, US President Donald Trump played fast and loose with reality in order to 'stir great collective passions', and his methods revealed a skilled performer at work. As Oscar Wilde asserted in his provocative dialogue, 'The Decay of Lying' (1889): 'Lying and poetry are arts – arts, as Plato saw, not unconnected with each other – and they require the most careful study, the most disinterested devotion'.[57] According to this way of thinking, President Trump may not have been merely the unsteady buffoon of much hostile commentary, but a sort of artist whose techniques should have been taken seriously. When we look at Trump's rise to power, we find a figure who, prior to becoming president, played the role of a successful businessman in the television programme *The Apprentice*. Like his Californian predecessor, Ronald Reagan, Trump consistently demonstrated a well-developed sense of the power of the theatrical, particularly at campaign rallies, which mixed fear and fun in a compelling combination. Trump's evolving sense of his own personal acting style could also be seen in a remarkable video from 2004, when Trump took part in an MTV concert that masqueraded as a political convention, during which Trump gave a speech endorsing the rapper Eminem for president.[58] Here, Trump could be seen rehearsing the gestures, verbal cadences and stylistic tics of his mature political style.

From the 1980s, Trump also involved himself with the performances of professional wrestling. One video from 2007 showed him participating in World Wrestling Entertainment (WWE) event, and developing the character for himself as the rich strongman who would fight on the side of the working class.[59] These events, and the television show *The Apprentice*, were of course heavily rehearsed, scripted and edited fictions. The self-sufficient businessman of *The Apprentice* was in fact a figure who had inherited a vast fortune from his father. The showman on MTV took part in an entirely pretend political convention. The bruiser of WWE participated in a performance event that

---

56 Ezra Pound, *Plays Modelled on the Noh*, ed. by Donald C. Gallup (Toledo: The Friends of the University of Toledo Libraries, 1987), p. 6.

57 Oscar Wilde, 'The Decay of Lying: An Observation', in *The Complete Works of Oscar Wilde: Volume 4: Criticism: Historical Criticism, Intentions, The Soul of Man*, ed. Josephine M. Guy (Oxford: Oxford University Press, 2007), pp. 73–103, p. 76.

58 The video can be seen embedded in Raisa Bruner's article, 'Donald Trump and Eminem Weren't Always Enemies. Here's Proof', *Time*, 11 October 2017, https://time.com/4978126/trump-eminem-endorsement/.

59 'Donald Trump Bodyslams, Beats and Shaves Vince McMahon at Wrestlemania XXIII', https://www.youtube.com/watch?v=MMKFIHRpe71.

purported to show fighting but which actually had a method somewhat akin to ballet choreography. Nonetheless, in each of these fictional scenarios, Trump honed, through his acting performances, a set of memorable characteristics and visually arresting images that would prove invaluable during his later political career.

The Washington Post detailed the way that Trump's political scripts for his successful election campaign appeared improvised and haphazard but were in fact carefully constructed, much like a literary drama. Some of Trump's key phrases, such as 'deep state' or 'drain the swamp', were tested in 2014 by the political-consulting firm Cambridge Analytica and by Trump's chief strategist, Steven Bannon, as part of a campaign of voter persuasion.[60] Trump himself, in one speech, self-perceptively described the development of such scripts:

They had this expression, 'drain the swamp', and I hated it. I thought it was so hokey. I said, 'That is the hokiest – give me a break. I'm embarrassed to say it'. And I was in Florida with 25,000 people going wild, and I said, 'And we will drain the swamp'. The place went crazy. [Laughter]. I couldn't believe it. And then, the next speech, I said it again. And they went even crazier. 'We will drain the swamp.' […] And every time I said it, I'd get the biggest applause.[61]

Such a performance is – at least according to some definitions – the sign of a very talented actor. After all, in the eighteenth century, Denis Diderot, who had a very different conception of actorly truthfulness than those who deploy 'method' acting techniques, asked: 'What, then, is a great actor? A man who, having learnt the words set down for him by the author, fools you thoroughly, whether in tragedy or comedy'.[62]

It is in this setting that Trump refined and popularized his usage of the term 'fake news'. From 2017, he consistently used the term in order to question

---

60 Craig Timberg, Karla Adam and Michael Kranish, 'Bannon Oversaw Cambridge Analytica's Collection of Facebook Data, According to Former Employee', *The Washington Post*, 20 March 2018, https://www.washingtonpost.com/politics/bannon-oversaw-cambridge-analyticas-collection-of-facebook-data-according-to-former-employee/2018/03/20/8fb369a6-2c55-11e8-b0b0-f706877db618_story.html?utm_term=.01dc0d5fa6ff.

61 Alex Leary, 'Trump: "And I Was in Florida with 25,000 People Going Wild"', *Tampa Bay Times*, 21 March 2018, https://www.tampabay.com/florida-politics/buzz/2018/03/20/and-i-was-in-florida-with-25000-people-going-wild/.

62 Denis Diderot, *The Paradox of Acting*, trans. by Walter Herries Pollock (New York: Hill & Wang, 1957), p. 33.

and undermine journalism from news organizations that contradicted or criticized the work of his administration. Ironically, he even made the false claim that he had invented the term, stating that 'fake news' is 'one of the greatest of all terms I've come up with'.[63] Furthermore, Trump, with his knowledge from pro-wrestling of how to rile up a crowd through theatrical displays of good and bad, and with his knowledge from *The Apprentice* of how to depict winners and losers, tended to place journalists and news cameras in a pen at the rear of his political rallies, with Trump then repeatedly gesturing at those reporters and insulting them as 'fake news', at the same time as his supporters booed and jeered. Through Trump, then, this modern term 'fake news' has an essentially theatrical and audience-focused genesis.

Crisis Actors

The day after Donald Trump launched his presidential campaign in 2015, the *Hollywood Reporter* noted that a casting call had been distributed the previous Friday, offering paid actors $50 to turn up as extras at the Trump event. The New York-based firm, 'Extra Mile Casting', sent an email advertisement declaring that an opportunity existed at an

> event in support of Donald Trump and an upcoming exciting announcement he will be making at this event [...]. We are looking to cast people for the event to wear t-shirts and carry signs and help cheer him in support of his announcement. We understand this is not a traditional 'background job', but we believe acting comes in all forms and this is inclusive of that school of thought.[64]

Characteristically, Trump's campaign manager subsequently denied that Trump had paid anyone to attend that event, and emphasized instead that 'Mr. Trump draws record crowds at almost every venue at which he is a featured speaker'.[65]

---

63 Trump in an interview with Mike Huckabee, 7 October 2017, quoted by Meg Kelly, 'President Trump Cries "Fake News" and the World Follows', *The Washington Post*, 6 February 2018, https://www.washingtonpost.com/news/fact-checker/wp/2018/02/06/president-trump-cries-fake-news-and-the-world-follows/?utm_term=.31e629caf8f4.

64 Emmet McDermott, 'Donald Trump Campaign Offered Actors $50 to Cheer for Him at Presidential Announcement', *Hollywood Reporter*, 17 June 2015, https://www.hollywoodreporter.com/news/donald-trump-campaign-offered-actors-803161.

65 Ibid.

Paradoxically, although the Trump campaign relied on professional actors in this way, suspicions of employing thespians were repeatedly made by supporters of Trump against political opponents. This particular variety of fake news is sometimes referred to as 'astroturfing', a term used to indicate that although an event may appear to have grassroots political support, those grassroots are manufactured, and those who appear to be 'regular' people who are motivated by a particular cause are, in fact, trained actors who are being paid.

At one extreme of this phenomenon lies a set of ideas about the 'crisis actor'. Actors have for many years been used to help train those involved in various public-service roles. For example, acting professionals are sometimes employed to help the emergency services and first responders to practice drills in case of a disaster situation. Such actors take on the role of mock victims, and may feign particular injuries, in order to add realism to a training situation, and to prepare firefighters, medics or police officers to deal with such a scenario in real life. However, that idea of the 'crisis actor' has, in recent years, been co-opted by conspiracy theorists, particularly online, who claim that such actors have been employed in order to present simulated disasters to the public as though real.

For example, after the appalling school shooting at Sandy Hook in 2012, conspiracy theorists who opposed gun-control measures claimed that the entire news story was simply untrue. The event was, they asserted, staged by gun-control advocates, using 'crisis actors'. Just as actors might simulate injuries during police training exercises, so troupes of 'crisis actors' had been hired in order to pretend to be the victims, the bereaved and the emergency services at Sandy Hook. According to this line of thought, a traumatized public was thus being manipulated into supporting restrictive legislation about the sale and ownership of guns. Such views were promoted by the prominent conspiracy theorist Alex Jones, who declared: 'If children were lost in Sandy Hook, my heart goes out to each and every one of those parents, and the people that say they're parents that I see on the news. The only problem is [...] I've seen actors before'.[66] His attorney also claimed that Jones himself was simply 'playing a character' and that Jones, although presenting an internet news platform called *InfoWars*, was 'playing a character. He is a performance

---

66 Quoted by Elizabeth Williamson, 'Truth in a Post-Truth Era: Sandy Hook Families Sue Alex Jones, Conspiracy Theorist', *The New York Times*, 23 May 2018, https://www. nytimes.com/2018/05/23/us/politics/alex-jones-trump-sandy-hook.html.

artist'.[67] Donald Trump, who appeared on Jones's show when campaigning for the presidency in December 2015 and declared 'Your reputation is amazing. I will not let you down', adopted similar tactics in claiming that his political opponents must be paid actors.[68] For example, Trump claimed that those who opposed his supreme court nominee in 2018 were 'paid professionals', and tweeted, 'The paid D.C. protestors are now ready to REALLY protest because they haven't got their checks – in other words, they weren't paid'.[69]

Here, then, the theatricalized notion of fake news sends observers down a rabbit hole. If those who present news shows are claiming to be performance artists and if the apparently real-life characters in political campaigns are accused of being paid actors, then it becomes increasingly difficult to know how to interpret the things that are being presented to us. Hyper-partisan reporting merges here with the entirely invented, and the two become indistinguishable. Thus the political sphere risks becoming a kind of Live Action Role Playing Game. Donald Trump's Orwellian way of dealing with this was to tell his supporters to trust only him, because 'what you're seeing and what you're reading is not what's happening'.[70] Today, then, it does not take long, when looking on the internet for information about high-profile current events, to find numerous unverified ideas, and the Trump-inspired approach is simply to believe or disbelieve the assertions you may find depending on your own pre-existing suspicions and the pronouncements of your favoured political leaders.

Vladislav Surkov

A sophisticated exploitation of this confusion can be found in early twenty-first century Russia, where the PR man Vladislav Surkov worked as one of President Vladimir Putin's key advisers until 2020. Surkov previously

67 Quoted by Will Worley, 'InfoWars' Alex Jones Is a "Performance Artist Playing a Character," Says His Lawyer', *Independent*, 17 April 2017, https://www.independent. co.uk/news/infowards-alex-jones-performance-artist-playing-character-lawyer-conspiracy-theory-donald-trump-a7687571.html.

68 Quoted by Jack Nicas, 'Alex Jones Said Bans Would Strengthen Him. He Was Wrong', *The New York Times*, 4 September 2018, https://www.nytimes.com/2018/09/04/technology/alex-jones-infowards-bans-traffic.html.

69 Donald Trump, Twitter message of 9 October 2018, https://twitter.com/realdonaldtrump/status/1049638803177127936?lang=en.

70 Donald Trump, 'Remarks by President Trump at the Veterans of Foreign Wars of the United States National Convention', Kansas City, 24 July 2018, https://www.whitehouse.gov/briefings-statements/remarks-president-trump-veterans-foreign-wars-united-states-national-convention-kansas-city-mo/.

attended Moscow Institute of Culture, spending three years there as part of
a five-year programme in theatre direction. But after he went to work for
the Kremlin, Surkov reapplied what he had learned in the theatre world.
As the filmmaker Adam Curtis has observed of Surkov:

> He came originally from the avant-garde art world, and those who
> have studied his career say that what Surkov has done is to import
> ideas from conceptual art into the very heart of politics. His aim is to
> undermine peoples' perceptions of the world, so they never know what
> is really happening. Surkov turned Russian politics into a bewildering,
> constantly changing piece of theatre. He sponsored all kinds of groups,
> from neo-Nazi skinheads to liberal human rights groups. He even
> backed parties that were opposed to President Putin. But the key thing
> was that Surkov then let it be known that this was what he was doing.
> Which meant that no-one was sure what was real or fake. As one
> journalist put it: 'It is a strategy of power that keeps any opposition
> constantly confused'.[71]

Peter Pomerantsev describes Surkov as having 'directed Russian society like
one great reality show. He claps once and a new political party appears.
He claps again and creates Nashi, the Russian equivalent of the Hitler
Youth'.[72] As Curtis notes, Surkov intended to create a 'defeatist response' that
has 'become a central part of a new system of political control', but which
has relied upon Surkov's prior knowledge of theatre. As Surkov himself put
it in 2021, 'I studied the *Commedia dell'arte*. There is a limited cast [...] they
represent all strata of society', and yet 'In this masked comedy, there is a
director, there is a plot. And this is when I understood what needed to be
done [...] We had to give diversity to the people. But that diversity had to be
under control'.[73]

Surkov also wrote (or is alleged to have written – his statements on the matter
are characteristically ambiguous) a bestselling novel *Almost Zero*, published
in 2009 under the pseudonym Natan Dubovitsky.[74] The novel repeatedly

---

71 Adam Curtis, *Bitter Lake*, Prod. Lucy Kelsall, BBC, 25 January 2015.
72 Peter Pomerantsev, *Nothing Is True and Everything Is Possible* (London: Faber, 2015), p. 77.
73 Quoted by Henry Foy, 'Vladislav Surkov: "An Overdose of Freedom Is Lethal to
    a State', *Financial Times*, 18 June 2021, https://www.ft.com/content/1324acbb-f475-
    47ab-a914-4a96a9d14bac.
74 Peter Pomerantsev, p. 82.

refers to Shakespeare's *Hamlet,* and at a central point in the novel, the main character Yegor Kirilovich (a kind of intellectual gangster who deals in literary manuscripts) is invited to watch a film that shows the murder of his former lover. Yegor is told:

> The studio 'Kafkas Pictures' shoots movies that look like legitimate films. However, the rape and torture scenes in their films aren't just realistic – they're real. They shot a version of Hamlet where all the characters – Hamlet, the Queen, the King, and Laertes – were actually killed. The actors were all killed during the filming, in their costumes and on set. Two of them, Hamlet and Laertes, were terminally ill volunteers who requested their next in kin to be paid in full. They gave their permission to be fatally wounded on camera. But two were tricked; they thought till their last breaths that there were just starring in a movie.[75]

In this description, Surkov's novel urges a reconsideration of the connection between performed drama and real life. Central to Surkov's description of *Hamlet* in *Almost Zero* is confusion about whether the audience is watching authentic murders, or whether those spectators are witnessing a fictional simulation. That mystery is wrapped inside the novel's broader enigma about the author's identity: at one stage Surkov declared 'The author of this novel is an unoriginal Hamlet-obsessed hack', but he also commented that 'this is the best book I have ever read'.[76]

Indeed, the innovation of Surkov and the other purveyors of fake news is to make a broader set of audiences unsure of whether they are watching a fictional drama or something that has really happened, and to remain completely unsure about who the authors of such events might be. Images of war, rebellion and destruction on the television news and on the internet are ubiquitous, but Surkov's technique makes an audience radically uncertain. If we believe that such sights have been staged or manipulated, then our capacity to be moved by them and to critique the situation in which they occurred may be diminished. Brecht felt that the danger of certain kinds of emotive drama was that it might dull the spectator's desire to change

---

75 Natan Dubovitsky and Vladislav Surkov, *Almost Zero*, trans. by Nino Gojiashvili and Nastya Valentine (RareAudioBooks.com), Kindle reader location 2159 of 3094.

76 Quoted by Peter Pomerantsev, 'The Hidden Author of Putinism', *The Atlantic*, 7 November 2014, https://www.theatlantic.com/international/archive/2014/11/hidden-author-putinism-russia-vladislav-surkov/382489/.

anything. Surkov's idea of drama is similar, that an audience might be dulled into inaction by confusion and cynicism.

The most famous stage direction of Samuel Beckett's play *Waiting for Godot* is the one which ends both the first and second acts of the play:

> **Estragon**   Well, shall we go?
> **Vladimir**   Yes, let's go.
> *They do not move.*
> CURTAIN[77]

Here, the words being spoken do not fit the action being taken. Indeed, the words directly contradict the action. In Beckett's play, the character of Lucky becomes dumb in the second act, Pozzo becomes blind, the vegetables become blackened and even language itself becomes decayed and pointless. In Russia, Vladislav Surkov took careful note of Beckett. Indeed, Surkov's novel *Almost Zero* begins with an introduction that address his readers directly, and which looks back to the setting and the characters of *Waiting for Godot*:

> Can everybody see the vast expanse of space into which walk a pair of clowns, a vulgar duo of charlatans, corrupt comics, masters of their craft – their craft simply teasing and mocking, tormenting and taunting – also, at any moment ready to perform tragedy, or pastoral, or something of ambiguity […] Two clowns emerge; their names Bim and Bom, Yin and Yang, Adam and Eve, Taira and Minamoto, Vladimir and Estragon […][78]

In 2011, Kirill Serebrennikov staged a four-hour-long adaptation of *Almost Zero* on the small 150-seat stage of the Moscow Arts Theatre, and the two clowns appeared on the stage (played by Alexei Kravchenko and Fyodor Lavrov) at the start of the performance, acting as hosts of the dark and comic performance that followed, and providing a Beckettian frame to the entire onstage action.[79]

Surkov's interest in Beckett potentially justifies an older, left-wing suspicion of the effect of Beckett's plays. As Raymond Williams puts it,

---

77 Samuel Beckett, *Waiting for Godot* (London: Faber, 1965), p. 94.
78 'Introduction', *Almost Zero*, by Natan Dubovitsky, Vladislav Surkov, trans. by Nino Gojiashvili and Nastya Valentine, Kindle Edition, location 37 of 3094.
79 Roman Dolzhansky, 'Lyrical Heroism', *Kommersant*, 17 January 2011, http://www.smotr.ru/2010/2010_tab_0.htm.

Beckett's theatre sets about 'converting a dynamism of form which had flirted with a dynamic of action to a repetitious, mutually misunderstanding stasis of condition'.[80] Surkov's political techniques seek to place the audience in a position analogous to Beckett's two main characters, Vladimir and Estragon, terminally unsure about what is going on, unable to decipher anything about the broader social structure of the situation, and left with a sense of the futility of action: that anything done or said will have little or no effect. We may as well simply tell one another jokes and play games to pass the time. In this way, theatricalized fake news might potentially do great damage to the citizen's willingness to take action, and thus to the participative structures of democratic society.

The cynicism of figure such as Surkov is likely to encounter still more technological opportunity in the future. As Franklin Foer pointed out in 2018, video manipulation techniques are on the verge of becoming so ubiquitous and so effective that the period in which visual evidence was widely trusted (to show things such as, say, the Rodney King beating) may soon start to look like a brief and bizarre historical period. Foer suggests, 'Fabricated videos will create new and understandable suspicions about everything we watch [...] manipulated video will ultimately destroy faith in our strongest remaining tether to the idea of common reality'.[81]

The inevitable response to such a situation may well be political scepticism and apathy. But it is important to highlight that there is an alternative tradition of performance which has a very different intention. Russia and the USA may be the home of Surkov, Putin and Trump, and may, in recent years, have been at the forefront of developing fake news in order to inspire political confusion and disengagement. But if we look slightly further back in history, we find that Russia and the USA have also developed a very different dramatic tradition, in which theatre makers have taken inspiration from the news media in order to inform spectators and to rouse the audience's capacity for action, albeit in a way that raises other questions about partiality and bias.

---

80 Raymond Williams, 'Theatre as a Political Forum', in Tony Pinkney, ed., *The Politics of Modernism: Against the New Conformists* (London: Verso, 1989), p. 94. Beckett himself was scarcely politically neutral: he joined the French resistance in the Second World War, and critics such as Emilie Morin have increasingly connected his drama with the politics that he experienced.

81 Franklin Foer, 'The Era of Fake Video Begins', *The Atlantic*, May 2018, https://www. theatlantic.com/magazine/archive/2018/05/realitys-end/556877/.

Hallie Flanagan and Living Newspapers

In 1919, the Central Committee of the Soviet Union Communist Party endorsed the idea of public readings of the news, accompanied by 'demonstrations', 'concert numbers' and projections of cinematic and magic lantern images.[82] The theatre director and poet, Mikhail Pustynin, is highlighted by Robert Leach as the key figure who developed the idea that 'news could be made more accessible through dramatization'.[83] Pustynin worked for the 'Blue Blouse Soviet Living Newspaper', a touring theatre company which invented the term *zhivaya gazeta*, 'living newspaper'.[84] Richard Drain explains what this 'living newspaper' style of performance implied: those planning such performances 'refused to use professional writers, but practised "lit-montage", ie. the scripts were cut-ups, principally of material from papers and magazines [...] staged them in revue style, performing in factories, workers' clubs and in the open air'.[85]

These 'living newspapers' were emulated by groups in many different countries, perhaps most notably in the USA. In 1935, the government of Franklin D. Roosevelt, struggling with the Great Depression, opted to set up the 'Federal Theatre Project' to employ jobless actors.[86] The project was directed at a national level by Hallie Flanagan, who had run an experimental theatre at Vassar College, and had travelled across Europe during the 1920s, when she had noted the way that, in the Soviet Union, theatre was being used to effect social change.[87] In her book *Arena*, Flanagan recalls suggesting that one way to set the many unemployed actors to work would be to 'dramatize the news without expensive scenery – just living actors, light, music, movement'.[88] The 'Living Newspaper' would use 'epic' techniques: the characters onstage were types rather than psychologically nuanced individuals; the pieces were constructed in episodic style rather than

82 John W. Casson, 'Living Newspaper: Theatre and Therapy', *The Drama Review*, 44:2 (2000), pp. 107–22, p. 108.

83 Robert Leach, *Revolutionary Theatre* (London: Routledge, 1994), p. 82.

84 Jordanna Cox, 'The Phantom Public, the Living Newspaper: Reanimating the Public in the Federal Theatre Project's 1935 (New York, 1935)', *Theatre Survey*, 58:3 (September 2017), pp. 300–25, p. 325.

85 Richard Drain, *Twentieth-Century Theatre: A Sourcebook* (London: Routledge, 1995), p. 183.

86 Jane DeHart Mathews, *Federal Theatre, 1935–1939: Plays, Relief, and Politics* (Princeton: Princeton University Press, 1967), p. 23.

87 Gerry Cobb, '"Injunction Granted" in Its Times: A Living Newspaper Reappraised', *New Theatre Quarterly*, 6:23 (1990), pp. 279–96, p. 284.

88 Hallie Flanagan, *Arena: The History of the Federal Theatre* (New York: Benjamin Blom, 1940), p. 65.

with a neatly developing plot, and there was use of music, direct address, film and slide projection. Such staging would 'attempt to create an authoritative dramatic treatment, at once historic and contemporary, of current problems'.[89]
Gerry Cobb observes:

If the rationale behind the Living Newspapers was news, however, its commitment was 'editorial', a preference for one side of the argument presented [...] In more precise terms, the Living Newspapers offered solutions to problems that were essentially political in nature and, generally speaking, supportive of the New Deal.[90]

John S. O'Connor argues that, if this perspective scarcely made the Living Newspaper project 'radical', the performances did nonetheless have a political effect:

The truth-telling quality of these productions exploded popular myths about the topic. They thus forced the public to see clearly a problem and its causes, often despite the public's preference to keep them hidden. The Living Newspapers showed that people did not live in slums because they were shiftless, that farmers were not poor because they were lazy or stupid, and that syphilis was not the physical verification of personal sin. Because it presented facts in a fresh, vivid and credible way, the Living Newspaper compelled the audience to respond to real social ills.[91]

In this way, the Living Newspapers took a clear editorial line. When the Federal Theatre Project produced *Triple-A Plowed Under* – a production that was watched, with reported approval, by Brecht – *The New York Times* complained that this:

frequently brilliant review of the American farmer's plight since the years of the World War violates one rule of a good newspaper story. It waxes editorial. It takes sides. It concludes by no uncertain implication that the farmer, the workingman and the middle-class consumer are the victims of capitalist speculators – in other words, the 'system'.[92]

---

89 Ibid.
90 Gerry Cobb, pp. 284–85.
91 O'Connor, '*Spirochette* and the War on Syphilis', *The Drama Review*, 21:1 (1977) pp. 91–98, p. 92.
92 Gerry Cobb, p. 296. B.C., 'The Play: The Living Newspaper Finally Gets under Way', *The New York Times*, 16 March 1936, p. 21.

Because the Living Newspaper incorporated an obviously editorial slant, and because the project was federally subsidized and dealt with issues that proved contentious at the time, the actors repeatedly found themselves drawn into controversy. Indeed, the very first Living Newspaper production of the Federal Theatre in New York had been scheduled for January 1936, but the US government intervened and prevented anything other than a dress rehearsal from being seen, because the play would include speeches by Haile Selassie and Mussolini, as well as a transcription of a broadcast by Roosevelt.[93] Although subsequent Living Newspaper performances did appear onstage, by 1938 the House Un-American Activities Committee had been established, in order to scrutinize allegations of communist activity in the USA, and found a target in Flanagan's work. She defended her Living Newspapers, declaring:

> You see, in the Living Newspaper, everything is factual. The records from which any Living Newspaper is taken are always open to all of you and to anyone. And I think it is rather a remarkable fact, gentlemen, that in the three years of the existence of the Living Newspaper, not one allegation has been made that the news were untrue. Nobody has ever proved that we have ever misquoted.[94]

Still, Congress refused to provide the continuing funds for the Federal Theatre Project, and this dramatic work finished at the end of June 1939.

Joan Littlewood

Nonetheless, that was not the end of the Living Newspaper. Theatrical innovators including Piscator and Boal also utilized the form, and, in the UK, Joan Littlewood learned of Hallie Flanagan's experiments.[95] Littlewood and her husband Jimmy Miller (better known later as Ewan MacColl) opted to stage a Living Newspaper with Theatre Union, a group that sought to combine left-wing politics with theatrical innovation. The production was first staged in Manchester during March 1940, called *Last Edition* and

---

93 Arthur Arent, 'Ethiopia: The First "Living Newspaper"', *Education Theatre Journal*, 20:1 (1968), pp. 15–31, p. 16.

94 Quoted by Eric Bentley, *Thirty Years of Treason: Excerpts from Hearings before the House Committee on Un-American Activities, 1938–1968* (New York: Viking Press, 1971), p. 28.

95 Ben Harker, 'Mediating the 1930s: Documentary and Politics in Theatre Union's *Last Edition* (1940)', in *Get Real: Documentary Theatre Past and Present*, ed. by Alison Forsyth and Chris Megson (Houndmills: Palgrave, 2009), pp. 24–37, p. 25.

comprised 20 scenes that discussed events in the tumultuous period from 1934 to 1940. Here, Littlewood and Miller dealt with topics including the abuse of Trinidadians by British colonial administrators, the exploitation of miners in Britain, the unemployment that followed the Wall Street Crash, the Spanish Civil War and the rise of Hitler.

Last Edition shows an ambiguous attitude towards the print media. On the one hand, the play highlights the bias and distortion of the existing newspapers. At one stage, for instance, a journalist introduces himself by declaring 'I represent the Press, Suppress, Oppress and Depress'; and another scene incorporates quotes from journalists who have misunderstood the political situation in Russia (one character quotes the 'Daily Telegraph [from] 1919' to declare, 'It is quite certain that the armed forces of the Bolsheviks cannot offer any serious resistance to organised and well-armed pressure').[96] Elsewhere, two newsboys shout about the frivolous material that they are selling and which distracts readers away from society's genuine problems, 'All the latest, murders, rapes and football scores'.[97] To endorse this point, two 'fashionable ladies' buy a newspaper in order to ignore the British hunger marches of the mid-1930s.[98] Finally, in the closing moments of the work, the play condemns 'The men who breed hatred through their press'.[99]

However, the play does also acknowledge the power of the press to achieve good and convey the truth. At one point, a narrator speaks over a scene featuring a married couple: the husband dwells on losing his job as a cotton spinner, whilst the wife reads a newspaper. The narrator declares:

> Anything good in the papers tonight [...] anything there with an offer of hope. Anything that might be a possible way out of your misery. (PAUSE) No, only the news that's always there: –
> The Loch Ness monster seen again.
> An actress suing for divorce.
> The Worthing Pier destroyed by fire.
> Salford man's assault on child.[100]

---

96 Joan Littlewood and Jimmy Miller, *Last Edition*, Ruskin College Oxford, Ewan MacColl and Peggy Seeger Archive, f. 54, f. 87. I am grateful to the Estate of Joan Littlewood c/o Rogers, Coleridge & White Ltd. for permission to reproduce lines from this play.

97 Ibid., f. 6.

98 Ibid., f. 15.

99 Ibid., f. 96.

100 Ibid., f. 7.

Nonetheless, the narrator then continues, 'But wait [...] here's something about the cotton situation. A plan for regulating prices [...] says that only such a drastic plan can save the trade of Lancashire'.[101] The newspapers do, then, despite their tendency to print frivolous nonsense, have the power to convey important information about the structure of society. Such power is particularly emphasized when a journalist tries to draw the attention of British Prime Minister Neville Chamberlain to the threat posed by Hitler:

> JOURNALIST.   Excuse me Sir. That chap Hitler has just sent his troops into the Rhineland and torn up the treaty of Locarno.
> CHAMBERLAIN (AS HITLER BEGINS TO SPEAK AGAIN)   Don't bother me. [...]
> JOURNALIST (MORE URGENTLY)   Excuse me Sir. He's threatened to send his troops into Austria and the Austrian people would like some assurance from you.
> [...] CHAMBERLAIN. No. Just ignore it![102]

In a metatheatrical moment, one of the play's characters explains the methods being used by the acting company, declaring:

> We haven't invented characters to make a play or played to please or stupify [sic] – we are actors – yes – but we have tried to live this story. We read of Gresford [a mine disaster in Wales during 1934] in the papers. We read the reports, the comments. – We give you the story as we found it. These things are true – not a word is false.[103]

The newspapers may often focus on the salacious and the misleading, and at times the press deserves condemnation along with other exploitative aspects of capitalism. Nevertheless, as *Last Edition* points out, journalists also have an important role in uncovering and conveying information that is 'true'. Indeed, the 'Living Newspaper' itself relies on editing and ordering those truths from newspapers in order to allow theatre audiences to consider the possibilities for wider societal change.

The British security service, MI5, had monitored Littlewood's work on *Last Edition* and at the start of the play's second run, in May 1940, police raided the theatre and arrested the authors, who were then found guilty of

---

101 Ibid.
102 Ibid., f. 64.
103 Ibid., f. 32.

giving an unlicensed public performance.[104] Nonetheless, Joan Littlewood later recycled the theatrical and political approaches used in *Last Edition* for her most fully achieved theatre work. When she produced her landmark play *Oh What a Lovely War* in 1963, Littlewood again relied on the techniques of newspapers, whilst continuing to critique and criticize those very newspapers. Much of the onstage effect of *Oh What a Lovely War* is achieved via the 'news panel', which comments on the action being performed onstage with facts and headlines about the war, culminating in the panel stating 'The war to end wars [...] killed ten million [...] wounded twenty-one million [...] missing seven million'.[105] Yet, at the same time, the play implies that the press may be complicit with the desire for war, and that salacious reporting may lead to terrible consequences. As the 'ever-popular War Game' begins, we find newsboys dashing across the stage declaring 'Special! Austria declares war on Serbia!' and 'Extra! Russia mobilises! Russia mobilises'.[106] Those excitable headlines reveal a journalistic tendency to find titillation in conflict, with the newspapers in the play joining in the cacophony of voices pushing towards conflagration, from which again the press can potentially make money. After all, later in the play we find a woman selling newspapers near to a line of injured soldiers, shouting, 'Star, News, Standard [...] First wounded arrive at Waterloo [...] Read all about it'.[107]

Gillian Slovo and the Tribunal Plays

By the end of the twentieth century, verbatim theatre had become a significant feature of the British theatrical landscape. A series of writers took inspiration from newspaper reporting in order to create plays that in turn critiqued the press and deliberately sought to tell the kind of stories that those playwrights felt the media had failed to communicate fully. These plays included Joint Stock's *Yesterday's News* (1976), about war in Angola, which relied on one of the company who devised the piece, Paul Kember, having been a former journalist on the *Liverpool Echo*.[108] Elsewhere David Hare's

---

104 See Richard Norton-Taylor, 'MI5 Surveillance of Joan Littlewood during War Led to Two-Year BBC Ban', *The Guardian*, 4 March 2008, https://www.theguardian. com/world/2008/mar/04/secondworldwar.past.

105 Theatre Workshop, *Oh What a Lovely War* (London: Methuen, 1992), p. 106.

106 Ibid., p. 12, p. 20.

107 Ibid., p. 40.

108 Max Stafford-Clark, 'David Hare & Max Stafford-Clark', *Verbatim Verbatim: Contemporary Documentary Theatre*, ed. by Will Hammond and Dan Steward (London: Oberon, 2008), pp. 45–76, p. 47.

The Permanent Way (2003) was inspired by an article about the Hatfield rail crash published in *The Guardian* by Ian Jack.[109] *The Colour of Justice*, a well-known 1999 work which examined the racist murder of Stephen Lawrence, was put together by Richard Norton-Taylor, who was security-affairs editor for *The Guardian* newspaper. Norton-Taylor described how theatre 'can be an extension of journalism'.[110] Verbatim theatre, he felt, 'has shown just how powerful and how complementary to journalism – in many ways how much more effective than journalism – the theatre can be'.[111]

The theatrical work of Norton-Taylor was commissioned by Nicolas Kent, who between 1984 and 2012 acted as Artistic Director of the Tricycle Theatre in Kilburn, North London. From 1994, Kent's playhouse gained a reputation for producing pieces like *The Colour of Justice* that he labelled 'tribunal plays', a form of verbatim theatre that took inspiration from real-life legal tribunals, with Kent's theatre-makers editing the tribunal material into a short and digestible form for playhouse production. Kent felt that such plays could achieve what newspapers could not do. He explained that his work was 'like a living newspaper' and declared, 'I think that people rather like coming to the theatre and spending two hours really examining an issue, listening to the arguments and coming to their own conclusions'.[112]

Indeed, Kent declared that the impetus for his work on verbatim had come from a desire to correct the problems with contemporary journalism. He described having gone to the Hague for the hearings into the Srebrenica massacre, and then returning home the following day to find that 'there was nothing in any newspaper except literally about fifty words in *The Financial Times* tucked away somewhere. And that was all the reporting there was'.[113]

More bullishly, David Hare claimed that verbatim theatre 'does what journalism fails to do' and that theatre makers 'don't have the bad record journalism has for misrepresenting people'.[114] Hare felt that the Iraq war (2003–11) had been initiated on the back of misleading assertions about

---

109 David Hare, 'David Hare & Max Stafford-Clark', *Verbatim Verbatim: Contemporary Documentary Theatre*, ed. by Will Hammond and Dan Steward (London: Oberon, 2008), pp. 45–76, p. 62, p. 57.

110 Norton-Taylor, 'Richard Norton-Taylor', in *Verbatim Verbatim: Contemporary Documentary Theatre*, ed. by Will Hammond and Dan Steward (London: Oberon, 2008), pp. 103–32, p. 122.

111 Ibid., p. 105.

112 Nicolas Kent, 'Nicolas Kent', in *Verbatim Verbatim: Contemporary Documentary Theatre*, ed. by Will Hammond and Dan Steward (London: Oberon, 2008), pp. 133–68, p. 162.

113 Ibid., p. 136.

114 David Hare, 'David Hare & Max Stafford-Clark', p. 71.

Saddam Hussein possessing 'weapons of mass destruction', and that the British and US press had failed sufficiently to interrogate those US/UK government claims. Hare thus declared:

It is certainly true that the recent much publicised flush of British drama on factual subjects is taken by many to be a response to the failures of the press. Audiences at this time of global unease want the facts, but they also want the chance to look at the facts together, and in some depth. Everyone is aware that television and newspapers have decisively disillusioned us, in a way which seems beyond repair, by their trivial and partial coverage of seismic issues of war and peace [...] The fact that journalism is too arrogant to recognise the crisis adds to the crisis.[115]

Nonetheless, when Hare created his own verbatim play, *The Permanent Way*, he was himself accused of misquoting the chief executive of the Great North Eastern Railway, an accusation that was reported in *The Times*. Hare responded:

I must admit it did make me laugh. Here I am, being held to account for one half-quotation based on a misunderstanding which I immediately corrected. Does anyone seriously imagine that journalists on Murdoch papers behave with anything like the same understanding or alacrity? If journalists were held to account for the truthfulness of the way they represent their subject in interview, then *The Times* would be nothing except apologies for what appears in *The Times*. In my experience newspapers are a rich mix of what people never meant combined artfully with what people never said.[116]

However, the problem with tribunal theatre is that it threatens to replicate the same kinds of bias as Hare identifies in the newspapers or in broadcast news. These plays may have been labelled 'tribunal' pieces, and Nicolas Kent may assert that 'The intention of a tribunal play is always, always to try to arrive at the truth without exaggeration'.[117] But the participants in a real-life courtroom are compelled to obey a set of relatively fixed rules about what kind of evidence can be submitted, how that evidence can be received and

---

115 David Hare, *Obedience, Struggle & Revolt* (London: Faber, 2005), p. 28.
116 David Hare, 'David Hare & Max Stafford-Clark', pp. 61–62.
117 Nicolas Kent, 'Nicolas Kent', in *Verbatim Verbatim: Contemporary Documentary Theatre*, ed. by Will Hammond and Dan Steward (London: Oberon, 2008), p. 155.

understood, and who can present various kinds of material. A 'tribunal' in the playhouse is not bound by the same kinds of legal considerations, and hence a verbatim drama can place characters who have never seen one another in real life together on the same stage space, or can place material from real life within an edited context that strongly steers the audience towards particular conclusions. Crucially, audience members are likely to be unaware of what editorial processes have taken place, and so remain unsure about where the sources are taken from, or how the original material has been selected and supplemented.

During a period of intense rioting in England during the summer of 2011, Nicolas Kent commissioned the South African writer Gillian Slovo to write about the events taking place.[118] Slovo, herself the daughter of a journalist, set about interviewing figures who had been associated in some way with the riots, and then pieced together parts of what they said in order to create her play *The Riots*. The real-life rioting finished after four nights on 10 August 2011, and Slovo's *The Riots* premiered in Kilburn's Tricycle theatre just three months later, on 17 November 2011. When Slovo was interviewed about *The Riots*, she described how she had chosen to make central to the play a representation of Mohammad Hammadoun, a real-life Tottenham resident who happened to be living above a 'Carpetright' store with his family when the building was burned down by rioters. Slovo said:

> [...] it was clear to me from the beginning, that we needed to hear from certain people, in particular I think we needed to hear from a victim, of the riots, and we needed some rioters, we needed some police, and out of those central [...] people [...] I built the story around them of the others [...][119]

Hammadoun was, in effect, auditioned and cast in a somewhat problematic role (a victim) which Slovo had imagined prior to the construction of her text. From a writerly point of view, this may make sense. But if Slovo is admitting 'I built the story', and approaching the issue with a narrative that she has already predetermined, even to the extent that she had delineated particular character types in advance, then there is a danger that this form of theatre replicates the problematic dynamic of journalism that some advocates of tribunal theatre believed the drama might displace. The playwright and

---

118   Aida Edemariam, 'The Cost of Survival', *The Guardian*, 5 May 2004, https://www.theguardian.com/world/2004/mar/05/southafrica.books.

119   'Playwright Gillian Slovo Talks about England Riots Play', *Front Row*, BBC Radio 4, 23 November 2011, http://www.bbc.co.uk/news/entertainment-arts-15856868.

actor Robin Soans had, after all, praised verbatim by contrast with newspaper reporting, saying,

> A journalist once told me that her editor, having already written his story, told her to 'Go out and find someone to say *such and such*'. With a fixed agenda like this, all a writer can do is fill in the gaps. When I work on a project, I may bring along my own preconceptions, but I try not to anticipate what I'm going to find before I get there.[120]

But as Sam Haddow points out, 'there is a tension operating at the heart of Slovo's praxis, where her protestations of objectivity and transparency appear to be hampering and even subverting the analytic or critical potential of the text itself'.[121]

Slovo responded to this kind of thinking in an interview on BBC Radio 4. When asked whether she was producing journalism or theatre, she responded:

> It is a play, though, because it's got actors, and it has to be a play-length, because audiences are paying to go and see it, and I consider it has to have an experience of being in the theatre. So it's verbatim but I'm not sure it's entirely a piece of journalism.[122]

Slovo's words were more nuanced than those spoken by many advocating this form of theatre, as she emphasized the hermeneutic importance of audience expectation. As Janelle Reinelt has put it: 'Audiences know that documents, facts, and evidence are always mediated when they are received; they know there is no raw truth apart from interpretation, but still, they want to experience the materiality of events'.[123] Thus, the 'tribunal' experiment can be seen as one of the latest in a series of innovative attempts by left-wing theatre makers to bring audiences towards a communal understanding of socio-political issues through drama. But there remain in those productions, which attempt to transcend or supplement conventional journalism, the very risks of distortion that thinkers of both the left and right have associated with the news media itself.

---

120 Robin Soans, 'Robin Soans', in *Verbatim Verbatim: Contemporary Documentary Theatre*, ed. by Will Hammond and Dan Steward (London: Oberon, 2008), pp. 15–44, pp. 29–30.

121 Sam Haddow, 'A Rebellious Past: History, Theatre and the England Riots', *Studies in Theatre and Performance*, 35:1 (2015), 7–21 (p. 12).

122 'Playwright Gillian Slovo Talks about England Riots Play', *Front Row*, BBC Radio 4, 23 November 2011, http://www.bbc.co.uk/news/entertainment-arts-15856868.

123 Janelle Reinelt, 'Towards a Poetics of Theatre and Public Events', *The Drama Review*, 50:3 (2006), pp. 69–87, p. 82.

Part Two

FAKE NEWS AND THE WESTERN DRAMATIC TRADITION

Truth, Falsehood and Theatrical History

Ever since there have been actors, there have been accusations that those actors are straightforward liars. Theatrical history traditionally tells the story of how the first European actor was a figure from more than 2,500 years ago called Thespis. He supposedly stepped out of the general singing and dancing of the chorus and addressed it as a character in his own right.

The techniques used by Thespis left him open to criticisms of lying. Diogenes Laerius records that the statesman Solon 'stopped Thespis from teaching tragedy, on the grounds that lying speech was unhelpful'. This encounter may be invented, but it is also recorded by Plutarch, who says: 'Solon saw Thespis acting his own parts as was the custom among those of earlier times. After the performance, he addressed Thespis and asked if he was not ashamed to tell so many lies in front of so many people'.[124]

The version of Solon depicted in Plutarch's narrative not only criticizes Thespis, but also criticizes the figure of Pisistratus. Pisistratus had wounded himself and then appeared in public claiming that his wound had been inflicted by 'enemies of the people', a resonant term that would be adopted in Shakespeare's *Coriolanus*, by Henrik Ibsen, and become intertwined with debates about fake news in the twenty-first century.[125] Solon apparently saw

---

124 Quoted by Elizabeth Irwin, *Solon and Early Greek Poetry: The Politics of Exhortation* (Cambridge: Cambridge University Press, 2005), p. 274.

125 For some explanation of the phrase's use in the twenty-first century, see Emma Graham-Harrison, '"Enemy of the People": Trump's Phrase and Its Echoes of Totalitarianism', *The Guardian*, 3 August 2018, https://www.theguardian.com/us-news/2018/aug/03/trump-enemy-of-the-people-meaning-history.

through Pisistratus's hoax, and said to man who pretended to be injured, 'You are not playing the part of Homeric Odysseus very well, son of Hippocrates'.[126]

Solon, then, reportedly disliked the activities of the first actor Thespis, and also censured those who might introduce theatrical techniques into the real world of politics, with Solon comparing the actions of Pisistratus to someone following a pre-prepared script. But, just as Donald Trump in our own day has criticized the 'paid professionals' who turn out for his opponents whilst employing actors at his own political events, so Solon was a clever theatrical thinker and an actor in his own right. Solon may have been ready to discover the theatrical duplicities of others because he himself had brought theatrical techniques into non-theatrical political contexts. When Solon was a young man, the Athenians had been fighting a war over the island of Salamis, but the fighting had been going so badly that they suspended the battle and passed a law that banned anyone, on pain of death, from mentioning the conflict. According to Plutarch, Solon knew that the general public nonetheless favoured a resumption of the fighting. So Solon hatched the kind of theatrical plan that is more familiar from the plot of Shakespeare's *Hamlet*. As Alex Gottesman puts it:

> People were not discussing it [the conflict over Salamis] because they were afraid of violating the law and thus no collective action was possible. But Solon had a plan. He first spread a rumour around the city that he was insane. This was important in setting the stage for his performance. Putting on a felt hat (perhaps signifying a convalescent state), he burst into the Agora, stood on the herald's stone, and broke out into an elegiac song he had composed and memorized about Salamis. 'A large crowd ran together'. The performance got people talking and led to public debates about the war; even Pisistratus himself spoke publicly in favour, presumably at an Assembly meeting. And thus the war resumed thanks to a theatrical stunt.[127]

Solon was scarcely the only figure in ancient Greece to consider the relationship between theatrical and political truth. In Sophocles' *Oedipus Rex*, the blind prophet Tiresias is described by the chorus as being the one in whom truth has been born, and he himself repeatedly uses the terms 'true' (*alêthes*)

---

126 Alex Gottesman, *Politics and the Street in Democratic Athens* (Cambridge: Cambridge University Press, 2014), p. 77.
127 Ibid.

or 'truth' (*alêtheia*). Indeed, King Oedipus at first introduces the prophet in exulted terms, as *anax* (king or lord). But Oedipus's view about this truthteller changes radically after Tiresias straightforwardly accuses Oedipus of patricide and indicates that Oedipus is engaged in an incestuous relationship. Oedipus responds to this information by accusing Tiresias of peddling fake news for profit, accusing the prophet of selling the story for wealth (*ploutē*). After all, as Patrick Finglass points out, 'Oedipus sincerely believes on the basis of personal experience that he knows this [Tiresia's information] to be false'.[128] Oedipus's pre-existing bias leaves him predisposed to reject the externally derived information, and, understandably, Tiresias has hardly been enthusiastic about conveying the news: indeed, Tiresias needs coaxing in order to pass Oedipus the information. The onstage chorus is left in a state of confusion, and as the piece continues the spectators are also left to make sense of the contradictory accounts of murder and attempted infanticide that are presented in the play. *Oedipus Rex* may have been written almost 2,500 years ago, but it presents a version of the modern dilemma facing democratic society: how can people in a functional society be brought to believe the same things about reality, and what starts to happen when trust in that shared reality begins to fray?

Questions about whether new information might be true or false, and how that information might affect rulers and those they govern, was therefore woven into the foundational drama of the Western tradition, and such questions are also found in some of the earliest criticism of the art form. Plato expressed a general suspicion of actors because he felt they were involved in something that essentially revolved around telling untruths, and he felt that actors often imitated bad behaviour such as lust and drunkenness, and might encourage others to copy such behaviour in real life. In broad terms, Plato's *Republic* raises the notion that poetic art, including drama, relies on *mimēsis* (imitation), which means the form is fundamentally separated from reality and so unable to tell the truth about that reality. More specifically, in the *Republic*, one of Plato's key objections to theatre is the effect it can have upon politics. If Solon could use theatrical techniques to rouse the mob, then Plato also spotted exactly this potential. Violent emotions could easily be incited in the theatre, as Plato put it:

> When many sit down together, in the assemblies, or the law courts, or the theaters, or the camps or any other public meeting place, and

---

128 Patrick J. Finglass, ed. and trans., 'Commentary', in Sophocles, *Oedipus the King* (Cambridge: Cambridge University Press, 2018), pp. 163–619, p. 268.

amid much noise they criticize those who say and do certain things, and praise those who say and do other things, both to excess as they shout and clap, and so on top of their noise the stones and the place where they are echo and double the racket of the blame and praise. Indeed, in such a scene how do you think a youngster's heart, as the saying goes, would be affected?[129]

Plato wrote that imitation appealed to the inferior part of the soul that was unconcerned with the truth: 'the imitator will have neither knowledge nor correct belief about the goodness or badness of the objects he's portraying', and that as a result, 'he'll imitate all the same without knowing in what respects the object is good or bad, but, it seems, the way it appears good to the ignorant masses is how he'll imitate it'.[130] In the *Republic*, then, Plato points out that people who create such fictions are ultimately in danger of creating audiences whose members are increasingly thoughtless. Although spectators may become invested in what they see, they may only be concerned with their sympathies being roused. Today, we find similar concerns about audiences who, through the enjoyment of online fake news, have their capacities for real understanding and analysis of information progressively worn down. As Plato puts it, theatrical imitations may not get to the truth of an issue because, 'that imitation is a kind of game and not serious'.[131]

However, although Plato may have been urging the public to be suspicious of performers, the *Republic* is itself set down in the form of a dramatic dialogue, with Plato inventing lines for the character of Socrates to deliver to a range of invented interlocutors. Hence, Plato was willing to assert that actors and poetic storytellers should not be trusted because of the effect they might have on others; yet, as Albert R. Spencer suggests, 'the dramatic Plato uses the *drama* of the dialogues to *experiment* with different line of inquiry in relation to specific *practical* problems'.[132]

In a similar way, Jesus Christ also condemned the way that theatrical techniques might introduce untruth into daily life, whilst also deploying a set of dramatic methods in his own public ministry. It is reasonable to suggest that Jesus himself may have watched a theatre show, and in the synoptic gospels (Matthew, Mark and Luke) the figure of Jesus has a predilection for using

---

129 Plato, *Republic: Books 6–10*, ed. by Chris Emlyn-Jones and William Preddy (Cambridge, MA: Harvard University Press, 2013), p. 33.

130 Ibid., p. 419.

131 Ibid.

132 Albert R. Spencer, 'The Dialogues as Dramatic Rehearsal: Plato's Republic and the Moral Accounting Metaphor', *The Pluralist*, 8:2 (2013), pp. 26–35, p. 30.

the language of the stage. According to the gospel accounts (of Mark 10:46 and John 4:3-6) Jesus's ministry saw him in the area of towns with theatres, including Jericho and Samaria, and in the 1980s a set of archaeological excavations dated the construction of a 4,000-seat theatre at the town of Sepphoris to around the time that Jesus grew up in nearby Nazareth.[133] Yet, if we look at the language of Jesus, we find that he is repeatedly concerned by the fact that the techniques of stage actors are being misapplied outside the theatre in order to mislead and lie. References to 'hypocrites' occur 17 times in the synoptic gospels, almost exclusively in the sayings of Jesus himself. The term Jesus is using in these accounts is a theatrical one: he uses the Greek term *hypokritēs* which means, straightforwardly, someone who plays a role on a stage. As Richard Batey puts it, the Jesus of the synoptics had identified that, for some people in day-to-day life, 'Out of a good deed which should be done in private they create a public spectacle, which themselves as director, producer, and star, bowing to the audience's applause'.[134] Instead of conducting such acting performances to impress other human beings, Jesus is anxious that, in daily life, people need only to please God, 'your Father who is in secret' (Matthew 6:18). For Jesus, the deployment of acting techniques in daily life can constitute a kind of falsehood, designed only to win the approval of other people. Of course, Jesus's own ministry depended on his own piety being seen by a large number of people: he preached in a variety of public forums, and was executed in a way that demanded public witness upon what Alexadra Poulain labels a 'vertical stage'.[135] Thus, although he condemned the misleading activities of everyday *hypokritēs*, his own fate and later reputation depended upon the application of certain theatrical techniques outside the Roman playhouse itself.

In the Middle Ages, European writers went much further in developing theatrical techniques to tell the Christian story, with mystery plays and morality plays emerging in order to explicate the connection between God and man for a largely non-literate population. Again, in those theological dramas, audiences encountered debates about the nature of truth and deception that resonate in our own era of fake news. For example, in the late fifteenth-century morality play, *Everyman*, the titular character meets a number of characters that he realizes have been lying to him. Everyman discovers that his own death is imminent and tries to find someone who will travel that final journey with him. He repeatedly reflects on the words 'trust'/ 'true'/ 'truly'

133 Richard Batey, *Jesus and the Forgotten City* (Grand Rapids: Baker, 1991), pp. 92–94.
134 Ibid., p. 86.
135 Alexandra Poulain, *Irish Drama, Modernity and the Passion Play* (London: Palgrave Macmillan, 2016), p. 2.

as he observes that various allegorical figures have now abandoned him despite their earlier assurances to the contrary. Beauty and Fellowship, for example, have spouted lies about their future commitments, promising to accompany Everyman to his grave when, in fact, they will scarper from him. A character like Fellowship is torn between his past promises and his present desires ('Promise is duty –/But, and I should take such a voyage on me,/I know it well, it should be to my pain').[136] Meanwhile, the character of Goods is, in the terms of Oliver Hahl, Minjae Kim and Ezra W. Zuckerman, 'publicly challenging truth as a prescriptive norm'.[137] Goods freely admits:

> [...] to thy soul Good is a thief;
> For when thou art dead, this is my guise –
> Another to deceive in the same wise.[138]

Paradoxically, then, although Goods is a malevolent character who admits to being deceptive and to leading people away from God's way, the audience may rather end up admiring him for being honest and straight-talking, at least when compared with the other duplicitous figures encountered by Everyman. In this way, Goods may prefigure the way that a modern politician who is clear about his disregard for honesty may appear more trustworthy than those public figures who claim to say or do one thing, but who are exposed – via the disclosure, say, of private email messages – as sometimes believing or acting upon quite contradictory principles.

Shakespeare, the most famous playwright in the English language, also anticipated some of today's thinking about fake news: namely, why might people prove so credulous when receiving information from dubious sources? The character of Richard III owes an evident debt to the earlier realm of medieval performance, spending his time clearly challenging truth as a prescriptive norm, much like a medieval 'Vice' character. In Shakespeare's play, characters such as Lady Anne have no problem in immediately recognizing Richard as a 'dissembler', with a 'false' heart and tongue, but they are nonetheless liable to trust him. Indeed, shortly after delivering

---

136 *Everyman*, in *The Norton Anthology of English Literature: Eighth Edition: Volume A: The Middle Ages*, ed. by Alfred David and James Simpson (New York: W. W. Norton & Company, 2006), pp. 463–84, p. 469.

137 Oliver Hahl, Minjae Kim and Ezra W. Zuckerman, 'The Authentic Appeal of the Lying Demagogue: Proclaiming the Deeper Truth about Political Illegitimacy', *American Sociological Review*, 83:1 (2018), pp. 1–33, p. 5.

138 *Everyman*, p. 473.

that critique of Richard, Anne *marries* him.[139] Richard's personality is echoed in other figures including Edmund in *King Lear*, Iago in *Othello* and Don John in *Much Ado*, who look like the self-evident liars they are, and yet are believed by otherwise sane and sober characters.

But of course, at the same time as exploring the process of lying, Shakespeare's theatre was being denounced for its own lies. An anti-theatrical tradition, based on the Biblical imperative 'thou shalt not bear false witness', described actors and playwrights as suspect figures because they invented and performed fictions for a living. In 1580, for example, Anthony Munday complained that, in the theatre:

> Our nature is led away with vanity, which the author perceiving frames himself with novelties and strange trifles to content the vain humors of his rude auditors, feigning countries never heard of; monsters and prodigious creatures that are not: as of the Arimaspie, of the Grips, the Pygmies, the Cranes, and other such notorious lies.[140]

Shakespeare's plays, however, acknowledge a more complex dynamic than Munday's criticism allows. Shakespeare reveals the power of dramatic techniques to establish false information, and we find this in various metatheatrical moments in his work: for example, in *Twelfth Night*'s garden scene where Malvolio finds that his lady apparently loves him, or at Dover cliff in *King Lear* where Gloucester apparently falls to his death. But it is in *Hamlet* that, during the 'Mousetrap' scene, we find theatre being used most clearly to interrogate principles akin to those of twenty-first century fake news. Here, Shakespeare shows theatre's ability to critique established narratives and to test the shared assumptions of an interpretative community, potentially exposing the false ideas upon which those collective values might be based.

Putting Media Misinformation Onstage

Shakespearean characters complain of 'base news-mongers' (*Henry IV, Part I*) or of 'some mumble-news' (*Love's Labour's Lost*), but the figures of his plays repeatedly wish to hear 'news' that will provide insightful information about what is going on in the world.[141] Hamlet, remember, dies wishing to 'hear

---

139 William Shakespeare, pp. 555–57.
140 Anthony Munday, 'A Second and Third Blast of Retreat from Plays and Theaters', in *Shakespeare's Theatre: A Sourcebook*, ed. by Tanya Pollard (Oxford: Blackwell, 2004), pp. 62–83, p. 78.
141 William Shakespeare, p. 1322.

the news from England', and 'what news?' is a question that resounds through the oeuvre, primarily referring to verbal reports that are delivered orally.[142] However, at around the time of Shakespeare's death, Europe witnessed a general increase in the number and variety of journalistic *publications*. In 1620–21, Dutch publishers in Amsterdam produced small broadsheets called *corantos* that were written in English and destined for sale in London bookshops and stationers. According to Nicholas Brownlees, 'Despite the almost total absence of domestic news, and the irregularity of their shipment to England in what climatically was a dreadful summer, the Dutch–English *corantos* were apparently successful'.[143] As Ian Donaldson puts it, these *corantos* consisted of 'reports, characteristically with a strong anti-Catholic bias, about current events in continental Europe. These in turn soon encouraged the production of similar publications by local syndicates in London'.[144]

The playwright Ben Jonson proved quick to satirize such syndicates, and his 1625 play *The Staple of News* shows a 'staple', or office run by a syndicate of newsmongers, which, as Richard Harp puts it, 'employs emissaries to circulate around town to procure the latest gossip to sell to costumers. Jonson is here satirizing journalism's chaotic beginnings where citizens will pay to hear any rumors, the more outrageous the better'.[145] Because the staple is driven by commercial concerns, it focuses upon 'news' that is novel rather than anything that is particularly accurate. Hence, in *The Staple of News*, the 'news' includes comically unlikely stories such as that 'an invisible eel' has been invented to sink ships, an 'alewife' has discovered the secret of 'perpetual motion' and that 'the Brotherhood of the Rosy Cross' has perfected the art of making perfume by 'drawing farts out of dead bodies'.[146] Yet the fact that the play begins with four gossips, Mirth, Tattle, Expectation and Censure, who urge the character of Prologue 'Look your news be new and fresh', may be, according to Jane Rickard, 'making the serious point that the public appetite for news is indistinguishable not only from its appetite for gossip but also from its appetite for theatre'.[147] Furthermore, although Jonson satirizes the idea of paying for news – it is a

---

142 Ibid., p. 833.

143 Nicholas Brownlees, *The Language of Periodical News in Seventeenth-Century England* (Newcastle: Cambridge Scholars, 2011), p. 33.

144 Ian Donaldson, *Ben Jonson: A Life* (Oxford: Oxford University Press, 2011), p. 395.

145 Richard Harp, 'Jonson's Late Plays', in Richard Harp and Stanley Stewart, eds, *The Cambridge Companion to Ben Jonson* (Cambridge: Cambridge University Press, 2000), pp. 90–102, p. 90.

146 Ben Jonson, *The Staple of News*, ed. by Anthony Parr (Manchester: Manchester University Press, 1988), p. 161, p. 164.

147 Ibid., p. 65; Jane Rickard, 'A Divided Jonson?: Art and Truth in "The Staple of News"', *English Literary Renaissance*, 42:2 (2012), pp. 294–316, p. 301.

'weekly cheat to draw money' according to his note to the reader – the resolution of the play comes with an accurate news report when one of the characters who was supposed dead is revealed to be alive.[148] Thus, as Rickard puts it, 'Jonson recognizes the potential value of accurate news reporting, just as he explores the potential problems of commercial news production'.[149]

By the time of the nineteenth century, as Laurel Brake puts it, we find 'the involvement of almost all Victorian writers with the periodical press, as contributors, editors and/or proprietors. The nature of "authorship" in the period almost inevitably included periodical publication as one source of readers and income, and a determining format'.[150] By the late 1890s, W. B. Yeats was complaining that 'dramatic journalism has had full possession of the stage in England for a century'.[151] For example, in that decade, George Bernard Shaw wrote on a range of topics for the *Fortnightly*, worked as music critic for *The World* and functioned as theatre critic for the *Saturday Review*.[152] Yet in his playwriting, Shaw felt happy to highlight the biased and destructive side of the press. In 1915, Shaw wrote *O'Flaherty, V.C.* to attack crude wartime sentiment, and presents a patriotic General speaking to an Irish Catholic soldier who is fighting for Britain. The General expresses incredulity that the soldier appears to know little about why the war is taking place, asking 'Dont you read the papers?'[153] In response, the soldier declares that 'There's not many newsboys crying the evening paper in the trenches', and points out that even if he did have access to the newspapers, he would not necessarily be any more enlightened.[154] The soldier describes the prejudiced 'way the English papers talk about the Boshes' and asks, 'Why should I read the papers to be humbugged and lied to by them that had the cunning to stay at home and send me to fight for them?'[155]

Shaw's hero, Henrik Ibsen, was capable of writing with similar cynicism about the distortions of the press. In 1886, Ibsen wrote the play *Rosmersholm*,

148 Ibid., p. 152.
149 Jane Rickard, p. 296.
150 Laurel Brake, *Subjugated Knowledges: Journalism, Gender & Literature in the Nineteenth Century* (Houndmills: Macmillan, 1994), p.xii.
151 New York Public Library, Berg Collection 64B6626, Yeats, William Butler Manuscripts Box, The Celtic Theatre, Holograph Draft of Proposal, Signed and Dated Coole Park Summer of '97. Quote reproduced by Roy Foster, *W.B. Yeats: A Life: 1: The Apprentice Mage* (Oxford: Oxford University Press, 1998), p. 184.
152 Michael Holroyd, *Bernard Shaw: The One-Volume Definitive Edition* (London: Vintage, 1998), pp. 184–85.
153 Bernard Shaw, *O'Flaherty, V.C.* in George Bernard Shaw, *Playlets*, ed. by James Moran (Oxford: Oxford University Press, 2021), pp. 145–70, p. 153.
154 Ibid.
155 Ibid., pp. 154–55.

which, as Sarah Balkin puts it, 'depicts a society where political efficacy requires abandoning ideals in favor of partisan, selectively truthful versions of reality constructed by the media'.[156] In the first act of *Rosmersholm*, the widower and former pastor, Rosmer, is visited by his dead-wife's brother, Kroll. Kroll is a political conservative, who wants to establish a newspaper to combat radical politics, and he asks Rosmer, who is known for his integrity, to act as editor. When Rosmer refuses, Kroll responds by asking if he can at least use Rosmer's name, because 'The rest of us are looked on as distinct party men. I am told they are even trying to brand me personally as some desperate fanatic'.[157] Rosmer nonetheless refuses, admitting to holding a set of contrary values including atheism, and an appalled Kroll starts to suspect that Rosmer might be supporting not only free thinking but also free love. Kroll's newspaper therefore denounces Rosmer (although not by name) as someone who confesses apostasy when the 'most opportune and [...] the most profitable moment has arrived'.[158] At the Rosmer house, the housekeeper is moved by 'all the nasty things there's supposed to be about him in the papers', whilst Rosmer condemns the duplicitous nature of the press for writing things 'they know there is not a single word of truth in – yet they write them'.[159]

Ibsen explored a similar theme in his 1882 play, *An Enemy of the People*, which tells of a doctor who discovers that a Norwegian town has a poisoned water supply. The mayor of the town, however, wants the doctor to stay quiet because the town depends on the spa waters and medicinal baths for tourism (Steven Spielberg's 1975 film *Jaws* would recycle the broad outline of the plot). The doctor has nonetheless written an article for the local newspaper in order to expose the problem, and act three of the play is set in the offices of the *People's Herald* newspaper, where the doctor reveals plans for his journalistic campaign. The editor of the newspaper, Hovstad, is at first excited by the idea of publishing the doctor's writing. Hovstad likes the idea of attacking the local politicians, telling the doctor that 'truth must come first'.[160] But this editor soon changes his mind: the town's mayor visits him to reassure him that the danger is limited, the price of fixing the problem would be very high and that there would be a great economic cost incurred by closing the baths for repair. The editor therefore refuses to publish the doctor's journalism, and instead prints a falsely reassuring story by the town's mayor.

---

156 Sarah Balkin, 'Rosmersholm', *Theatre Journal*, 63:3 (2011), pp. 455–47, p. 455.
157 Henrik Ibsen, *Rosmersholm*, in Ibsen, *Ibsen: Volume VI*, trans. and ed. by James Walter McFarlane (Oxford: Oxford University Press, 1960), pp. 289–422, p. 304.
158 Ibid., p. 348.
159 Ibid., p. 366, p. 348.
160 Henrik Ibsen, *An Enemy of the People*, in Ibsen, *Ibsen: Volume VI*, trans. and ed. by James Walter McFarlane (Oxford: Oxford University Press, 1960), pp. 19–126, p. 47.

Hovstad declares that, ultimately, the newspaper should reflect rather than challenge the views and interests of its readers: 'Dr. Stockmann has public opinion against him. But what is the first and foremost duty of an editor, gentlemen? Is it not to work in harmony with his readers?'[161]

In return for telling the truth, the doctor in Ibsen's *An Enemy of the People* finds himself condemned, made a pariah and his house smashed; and Bertolt Brecht showed the similar ruination of a truth-telling scientist when he began working on his *Life of Galileo* in 1938. In one version of Brecht's text, Galileo declares, 'however many truths science knows, it could have no future in a world of lies'.[162] Yet, for Brecht, the media did not necessarily oppose such veracity, but could in fact aid the kind of truth-telling mission that powerful politicians might distrust. In Brecht's 1941 play, *The Resistible Rise of Arturo Ui*, we find a relatively positive appraisal of newspaper reporters. The reporter 'Ted Ragg' may be '*slightly drunk*' but speaks intelligently, and annoys Arturo Ui (a version of Adolf Hitler), by pointing out the transitory nature of Ui's fame. Ui complains that 'Those bastards/ Treat me like dirt' and demands that his bodyguards 'Shut/ Him up!' Ragg in turn issues the warning, 'Be careful, Ui. Don't insult/ The press'.[163]

Ui subsequently attempts to destroy the newspapers that speak out against him, and particularly focuses on the character of Dullfeet (a version of the real-life Austrian Chancellor, Engelbert Dollfuss), who runs a journal that makes accurate accusations against Ui's circle. In response, Dullfeet finds that his printing presses are smashed, and Ui himself makes an explicit request:

Ui [...] Your paper should stop printing these horror stories
That only make bad blood. I don't believe
I'm asking very much.
Dulfeet It's easy not
To write about what doesn't happen, sir.
Ui Exactly. And if now and then some trifling
Incident should occur, because the earth
Is inhabited by men and not by angels
You will abstain, I hope, from printing lurid
Stories about trigger-happy criminals.[164]

---

161 Ibid., p. 92.
162 Bertolt Brecht, *Life of Galileo*, trans. by John Willett, ed. by John Willett and Ralph Manheim (London: Methuen, 2001), p. 191.
163 Bertolt Brecht, *The Resistible Rise of Arturo Ui*, trans. by Ralph Manheim, in John Willett and Ralph Manheim, eds, *Brecht: Collected Plays: Six* (London: Methuen, 1994), pp. 353–70, pp. 135–36.
164 Ibid., p. 195.

This exchange was based upon the fact that, before being assassinated by Nazis in 1934, the real-life Austrian Chancellor Dollfuss felt coerced into agreeing to stop the attacks on Hitler that appeared in the Austrian press. Accordingly, in Brecht's play, Dullfeet is killed after this meeting with Ui. For Brecht, then, the press had a potentially noble but dangerous role, of revealing the truth that politicians may be desperately keen to keep from public view. Ibsen showed how newspapermen might be corrupted by meeting with a politician who persuades them to avoid printing unfavourable news. Brecht showed a similar process of political interference taking place, although Brecht gave more emphasis to the value of an independent press and the murderous threat sometimes faced by journalists.

A less flattering view of journalists and their interactions with politicians featured in the popular American drama, *The Front Page*, which opened in New York in 1928. This script was written by two former journalists who would go on to forge careers in Hollywood, Ben Hecht and Charles MacArthur, and it helped to fix many popular ideas about newspapermen, particularly as the drama inspired film versions in 1931, 1974 and 1988. *The Front Page* is a dark comedy, set on the eve of a convicted murder's hanging, and shows the tough, cynical newspapermen who are covering the crime beat. In this play, journalism is a realm of drink and danger, likely to leave reporters badly paid, lacking in humanity and vicious in pursuit of a story. The journalists at one stage demand information from one woman with the words, 'Come on, you lousy tart! Before we kick your teeth out!'[165] At one point these men invent a sex scandal involving a kind-hearted woman, who complains that she is traduced 'Just because you want to fill your lying papers with a lot of dirty scandal'.[166] The worst newspaperman of all is the editor of Chicago's *Herald Examiner*, who is happy to lie, see people killed and have one of his own journalists arrested on concocted charges in order that the newspaper succeeds against rival publications.

In *The Front Page* the world of newspapers is closely connected with that of politics. Journalists may expose the corruption of local politicians, who set about 'Hanging an innocent man to win an election' and who would 'kill your Mother to get elected'.[167] But the journalists are also incestuously connected with those same politicians, as shown when the reporters from rival Chicago

---

165 Ben Hecht and Charles MacArthur, *The Front Page* (New York: Samuel French, 1950), p. 98.
166 Ibid., p. 41.
167 Ibid., p. 135.

publications interact with a Republican politician, the Sheriff, to conspire over the proposed timing of the hanging of a man:

Bensinger   [...] how about hanging this guy at five o'clock instead of seven? It ain't going to hurt you and we can make the City Edition.

Sheriff   Aw, now, Roy, that's kind of raw. You can't hang a fella in his sleep, just to please a newspaper.

Murphy   (*Crosses to Center*) No, but you can reprieve him twice so the hanging'll come three days before election. So you can run on a law and order ticket!

[...]

Sheriff   All right, you'll just get scooped. Now we're going to reform these Reds with a rope. That's our slogan. (*To ENDICOTT*) Quote me if you want to. 'Sheriff Hartman pledges that he is going to reform the Reds with a rope'.

Endicott   Oh, for God's sake, Pinky! We've been printing that chestnut for weeks![168]

As in the work of Ibsen and Brecht, the troubling intersection of the political and the journalistic is probed here, with the Sheriff of *The Front Page* engaging in what would later be called 'media management'.

The Late Twentieth-Century Newspaper Industry

Sarah Kane's 1995 play *Blasted* presents a tabloid journalist called Ian who inhabits a zone where some kind of war is in progress, but the audience never really becomes aware of what is going on in this conflict, what the battle might be about, nor who is doing the fighting. There is therefore an overall failure of reporting in this situation, and eventually Ian is asked by a soldier – in a line that echoes one from Beckett's *Waiting for Godot* – to 'Tell them you saw me'.[169] But Ian apologizes to the soldier that he cannot do this; he is not a war reporter: 'I do other stuff. Shootings and rapes and kids getting fiddled by queer priests and schoolteachers. Not soldiers screwing each other for a patch of land'.[170]

---

168 Ibid., pp. 45–47.
169 Sarah Kane, *Complete Plays* (London: Methuen, 2001), p. 48.
170 Ibid.

In *Blasted*, Ian justifies his rationale for the kind of journalism that he carries out: his work is merely the creation of 'stories. That's all. Stories', and he only writes stories that people want to hear. As he puts it, 'No joy in a story about blacks who gives a shit?'[171] But moments after he explains his journalistic principles in this way, Ian's metaphorical blindness becomes a literal blindness, as the soldier rapes him and bites out Ian's eyes.

Kane's remarkable and era-defining play draws upon a number of theatrical ideas, pointing towards Ibsenite realism at the start and culminating in something distinctly Beckettian. But one of the traditions within which the play operates, and that is less well recognized, is the lineage of late twentieth-century British plays that attack news reporting in direct terms. Kane may provide an in-yer-face extreme of violence, but the critique of journalism in *Blasted* is also a culmination of the kinds of ideas that had been discussed by British dramatists during the years before her play appeared. For example, during 1971, the playwright Arnold Wesker spent two months in the Fleet-Street offices of the *Sunday Times*, and he subsequently wrote an essay about his time there. The *Sunday Times*'s journalists disputed the facts of this piece, and he was compelled to withdraw the essay from publication for half a decade. Those reporters felt hostile towards an essay that described 'the communication of objective fact' as being journalism's 'great myth'.[172] After all, Wesker's essay declared, 'as I write this piece, I make the discovery of what it must sometimes *feel* like to be a journalist – a shit!'[173]

As Sarah Lonsdale points out, Wesker had come to research the *Sunday Times* after a series of poor newspaper reviews of his play *The Friends* (1971).[174] Motivated by feelings of affront, Wesker created not just his essay but also a play, *The Journalists* (1972), which he claimed, 'is about the poisonous need to cut better men down to our size'.[175] But the play also focuses heavily on media distortions. The epic form of his play was designed to show that the subjective choices of journalists have a deleterious effect on how the wider public views the world. *The Journalists* is set on a Sunday newspaper, and shows how each department manifests its own biases and

---

171 Ibid.
172 Arnold Wesker, *Journey into Journalism* (London: Writers and Readers Publishing Cooperative, 1977), p. 105.
173 Ibid., p. 74.
174 Sarah Lonsdale, *The Journalist in British Fiction and Film* (London: Bloomsbury, 2016), p. 229.
175 Arnold Wesker, *The Journalists*, p. 9.

preferences, which give the reader a contorted sense of reality. As one of the journalists declares:

> cigarette packets carry a notice saying: 'Warning! Smoking can damage your health!' But what about all the newspapers carrying a notice on the front page, just below their names, saying: 'Warning! The selective attention to data herein contained may warp your view of the world!'[176]

In one of the central moments of Wesker's play, an in-depth investigative team abandons a worthy story about the resilience of bridges in order to pick up a more salacious story about a female doctor who has refused an abortion for a teenage girl:

Julian   And basically what you want is all the dirt I can get on her?
Mary   Yes. And get photographs of the girl and her mother. Doorstep them if necessary.
Julian   How can you take a moral position about the gynaecologist if you start invading people's privacy?
Mary   I'll worry about that.[177]

Wesker's play has never become widely known: it requires a cast of 30, and when it went into rehearsal at the RSC in 1972, the actors refused to perform it. Wesker believed this refusal was because 'The characters included four intelligent Tory cabinet ministers. That was absolutely verboten'.[178]

A better-known large-scale play that condemns the British newspaper industry in its late twentieth-century pomp is David Hare and Howard Brenton's *Pravda* (first staged at the National Theatre, London, in 1985). Brenton and Hare named the work after the official newspaper of the Soviet Union's Communist Party, but the action of the play was motivated by Rupert Murdoch's purchase of his first British broadsheet, *The Times*, in 1981. The play revolves around a nefarious fictional version of Murdoch, Lambert Le Roux (first played by Anthony Hopkins), who seizes a British regional title,

---

176   Arnold Wesker, *The Journalists, The Wedding Feast, Shylock* (London: Penguin, 1990), p. 101. Wesker repeated almost exactly the same words in his essay, *Journey into Journalism*, p. 106.

177   Ibid., p. 79. This exchange was apparently based on what happened in the real-life *Sunday Times* newsroom. See Magnus Linklater, 'Slog Times, All the Time', *The Observer*, 29 December 1991, p. 43.

178   John O'Mahony, 'Piques and Troughs', *The Guardian*, 25 May 2002, https://www.theguardian.com/books/2002/may/25/arts.artsfeatures.

the *Leicester Bystander,* before taking over the national, established newspaper, the *Daily Victory.* In the process, Le Roux spreads corruption and lies amongst all of those with whom he comes into contact.

However, the satire in *Pravda* is not only focused on the Murdoch figure of Le Roux: the world of news journalism is evidently corrupt and dishonest even before Le Roux takes charge. Towards the start of the play, a reader arrives at the officers of the *Leicester Bystander* to ask for a correction. The newspaper has incorrectly claimed that she has a son who is a drug dealer, although the woman has no son, and as a result customers are boycotting her small business. The deputy editor of the newspaper tells her:

Andrew   I honestly can't comment on the facts in this case.
Moira   It's a simple thing. It's a couple of lines. Please publish a
correction.
Andrew   Look I'll be frank [...] it isn't very easy [...] a newspaper
isn't just a scrap of paper, it's something that people feel they
have to trust. And if they can't trust it, why should they read it?
A thing is true or it isn't. So by definition, what is printed must be
true – otherwise why print it? And if we apologise and correct, how
can the readers know what is true and what is not?[179]

The editor of the newspaper, Harry Morrison, explains, before the Le Roux takeover, how even the rise of a political demagogue can be extremely good for the newspaper business. Morrison boasts, 'Hitler worked out very well for the *Bystander.* Because we saw him coming. It enhanced our reputation'.[180] Once the Murdoch-like figure of Le Roux arrives, however, the news business moves closer towards something that is almost satanic: indeed, the original stage production began with an opening that described Le Roux as 'that monster, that Satan'.[181] The closing line of the play sees Le Roux declaring: 'Welcome to the foundry of lies'.[182]

Tom Stoppard expressed some of Wesker, Hare and Brenton's cynicism in *Night and Day* (premiered in 1978, at London's Phoenix Theatre), which revolves around the foreign correspondent of a fictional newspaper, the *Sunday Globe.* One character, for example, complains that 'the whole thing gets misreported'; *The New York Times* is dismissed as 'All writing and no facts';

179 David Hare and Howard Brenton, *Pravda,* rev. edn (London: Bloomsbury, 2015 [1986]), p. 17.
180 Ibid., p. 13.
181 David Hare and Howard Brenton, *Pravda* (London: Methuen, 1985), p. 9.
182 David Hare and Howard Brenton, *Pravda* (rev. edn), p. 113.

and one political leader criticizes the British press for 'giving the reader as much of the truth as they think is good for him'.[183] Journalists are liable to be manipulated by governments. For example, when a press officer acting for the regime of a fictional country learns that the *Sunday Globe* is supposedly 'an objective fact-gathering organization' the press officer replies 'yes, but is it objective-for [the government] or objective-against?'[184] Another character worries that the realm of journalism is equally likely to be accused of being manipulated by business, as he states that the '*Globe* is a million packets of journalism manufactured every week by businessmen using journalists for their labour'.[185] One fictional African leader complains that 'a newspaper is not like a mine, or a bank, or an airline; it is the voice of the people and the Kambawe paper was the voice of an English millionaire'.[186]

Nonetheless, Stoppard has decidedly more sympathy towards the realm of newspaper reporting than Kane, Wesker, Hare and Brenton. After all, Stoppard had been employed in journalism from 1954: having left school at 17 he worked at Bristol's *Western Daily Press* for four years, before moving to the *Bristol Evening World* for another two.[187] As he puts it, 'I stopped being a journalist because I wanted to write plays, but I missed journalism. Both ambitions co-existed for quite a long time'.[188] In *Night and Day* we therefore find young journalist Jacob Milne, who justifies his profession by declaring:

Milne   [...] No matter how imperfect things are, if you've got a free press everything is correctable, and without it everything is concealable.
Ruth   I'm with you on the free press. It's the newspapers I can't stand.
Milne   [...] Junk journalism is the evidence of a society that has got at least one thing right, that there should be nobody with the power to dictate where responsible journalism begins.[189]

Towards the end of the play, one of Stoppard's characters reflects, 'I've been around a lot of places. People do awful things to each other. But it's

---

183 Tom Stoppard, *Night and Day*, in Stoppard, *Tom Stoppard Plays 5* (London: Faber, 1999), pp. 247–359, p. 271, p. 275, p. 341.
184 Ibid., p. 273.
185 Ibid., p. 312.
186 Ibid., p. 342.
187 Tom Stoppard, 'My Love Affair with Newspapers', *British Journalism Review*, 16:4 (2005), pp. 19–29, pp. 19–20.
188 Ibid., p. 23.
189 Tom Stoppard, *Night and Day*, p. 315.

worse in places where everybody is kept in the dark. It really is. Information is light. Information, in itself, about anything, is light. That's all you can say, really'.[190]

Post-Trump Drama

Those British dramas written between the 1960s and mid-1990s now feel dated because the media landscape has profoundly transformed in the wake of the disruptive power of the internet. But there is one play of that era, by the US writer Lorraine Hansberry, which contains a sophisticated and still pertinent critique of the media industry. Hansberry began writing her play *Les Blancs* in 1960, and although it remained unfinished at the time of her death in 1965, her executor and former husband Robert Nemiroff edited the script and a version first appeared onstage at New York's Longacre Theatre in 1970. The play revolves around a fictional African country whose people are struggling for independence in the 1960s, and where one visiting figure is a young, white, male American journalist. This journalist believes that 'It's easier when you are outside a situation to see the whole' and that he enjoys 'a particular kind of vantage point given to an outsider'.[191] However, by the end of the play he is schooled in the fact that even the apparently neutral observer cannot escape participating in colonialism. He is informed by one white medic that newspapers will report on the specific violence of anticolonial uprisings and 'the press of the world will send a shudder through men everywhere', but that 'colonial subjects die mainly from a way of life' which is legitimized by even helpfully meant European and US interventions. As the medic tells the journalist, a healthcare mission in Africa may focus on 'the incidentals – gangrene, tumours, stillborn babies' but overall 'Our work', with its long-established hierarchies, 'reinforces a way of life'.[192] Lurid details may 'send a shudder' through newspaper readers, but may in fact obscure the broader truth about situations such as colonialism and systematic exploitation.

In 2006, Facebook introduced its News Feed and Google launched its news app. In this internet age of news aggregation and personalized, algorithmically ordered content, theatrical depictions of media falsehoods tended to follow Lorraine Hansberry in emphasizing the vulnerability of the entire newsgathering enterprise, and the way that a profusion of reported

---

190 Ibid., pp. 354–55.
191 Lorraine Hansberry, *Les Blancs*, final text adapted by Robert Nimiroff (London: Samuel French, 1972), p. 56.
192 Ibid., p. 113.

details may obscure, or exist in contrast to, broader truths. For example, in 2013, Lucy Kirkwood's play *Chimerica* premiered at the Almeida Theatre in London, before transferring to the Harold Pinter Theatre. Kirkwood's work revolves around a fictional photojournalist, Joe Schofield, who, at the time of the 2012 US presidential election, was investigating the fate of the 'Tank Man', the Chinese protestor who had famously halted a line of tanks during the Tiananmen Square massacre of 1989. The play touches on how the Chinese authorities had suppressed news of pro-democracy protests, with one character saying of a teenage Chinese woman, 'She wasn't born when Tiananmen happened, it's been erased from the history books'.[193] But the play also points to the diminishing abilities of the Western media to research stories. When Joe speaks to his editor, at a fictional version of *The New York Times*, about a potential article on the 'Tank Man', his boss replies:

Frank   It's a great idea, boys, I can see why you're excited, but I don't have the money for this.

Joe   You don't have money for one of the great heroes in twentieth-century history?

Frank   I don't even have the money for our food critic to review anywhere you don't BYOB.[194]

The story about 'Tank Man' is definitely closed down by Frank after the company that owns the newspaper starts to seek investment capital from China, and as the editor puts it, 'when you owe a guy one-point-three trillion dollars it's prudent not to make a big deal out of the fact he knocks his wife around a little'.[195]

Frank subsequently complains about the twenty-first century media environment:

I suffer too! You think I enjoy using the word "multi-platform"? That I think it's *desirable* to employ the best writers in the country, then stick a comments section under their articles, so whatever no-neck grain-fucker from Arkansas can chip in his five uninformed, misspelled, hateful cents because God *forbid* an opinion should go unvoiced? Assholes Anonymous validating each other in packs under my banner, that's not a democratic press, it's a nationwide circle-jerk for imbeciles.[196]

---

193   Lucy Kirkwood, *Chimerica* (London: Nick Hern, 2013), p. 49.
194   Ibid., p. 31.
195   Ibid., p. 80.
196   Ibid., p. 81.

Kirkwood subsequently revised her script for a televised version of *Chimerica* in 2019. Her revised drama located the action during the election of Donald Trump, as Trump bans reporters from his rallies and castigates the 'Fake News Media'. This time the photojournalist at the heart of the story is a more compromised figure: he has digitally manipulated a photograph by splicing together two almost simultaneously taken images from the war in Syria. This forgery is discovered, he loses his job in disgrace and his quest to find 'Tank Man' is in part an effort to restore his reputation. The photojournalist's editor insists that the forgery is particularly egregious during the era of Trump, insisting, 'I have to call every editor in the country and apologize, because you have made all of us look dirty right at the moment we need more than ever to be immaculate. You have played right into his [Trump's] tiny hands'.[197] Nonetheless, the photojournalist continues to insist that, although the image may have been manipulated, it does represent a broader truth: 'It was real. It happened [...] apparently it's the only way to get Syria on the front page of this newspaper. Week after week I send you unthinkable atrocities and you bury them on page twelve'.[198]

This same dilemma occurs in Jeremy Kareken, David Murrell and Gordon Farrell's play *The Lifespan of a Fact*, which opened at New York's Studio 54 in October 2018. The play dramatizes the conflict between a fact-checker (originally played by Daniel Radcliffe) and a renowned writer. The play, based on real-life experience, revolves around a high-end magazine, whose managers are struggling to cope with an era of online content and are desperately chasing advertising revenue. The editor-in-chief has presided over a restructure where the fact-checking department has been abolished. In this environment, we see an eminent writer called John D'Agata, who is writing a piece for the magazine about a teenage suicide in Las Vegas, which promises to make an impact way beyond its ostensible subject matter by addressing modern isolation. However, the article is riddled with small fictionalizations, because D'Agata takes liberties in order to make his piece literary and artful.

D'Agata comes into conflict with the young fact-checker whom the magazine editor assigns to do a perfunctory check on the piece, but who identifies a long list of corrections. The fact-checker maintains that the writer

197 Lucy Kirkwood, *Chimerica*, episode 1, Channel 4, 17 April 2019.
198 Ibid. Kirkwood would go on to work on the HBO television drama, *Succession* (2018–), which is loosely based on Rupert Murdoch's family and media empire.

should stick entirely to the rational world of the provable. As he maintains, even a small fictionalization can lead to the overall piece being mistrusted:

> When the blogs and the fan sites and Twitter and 4chan and Reddit and whatever in the whole, insane Internet − when they start tearing you down brick by red fucking brick, they're not going to say 'Wow, John D'Agata altered certain details in the service of poetic truth', theyre going to say, 'Wow, John D'Agata lied'.[199]

Ultimately, the play asks, in an era when magazines are desperately pursuing readers and cannot usually afford detailed fact-checking, would it be better for editors to publish an essay that is illuminating a profound truth but is inaccurate in some of its detail, or would it be better to publish something entirely factual but vacuous such as a replacement article about 'Congressional Spouses'?

Elsewhere, James Graham premiered *Ink* at London's Almeida in June 2017, and the play, like Brenton and Hare's *Pravda*, focuses on the work of Rupert Murdoch. But if *Pravda* showed Murdoch sweeping all before him, *Ink* has a slightly different emphasis. Yes, by the end of Graham's play, Murdoch's tabloid newspaper the *Sun* is triumphant, corralling all of its rivals into an identikit range of editorial priorities, forcing competitors to take notice of 'legs, and, and boobs. And bums, bums, I like bums'.[200] Yet, at the same time, *Ink* indicates the vulnerability of the *Sun*'s approach. One rival editor cautions against 'Playing to people's fears, their hatred, and anger' because that would have led, in the past, to support for appeasement and slavery.[201] *Ink* also indicates that the *Sun* is ultimately likely to be superseded by a later era of social-media and user-generated content. As Murdoch puts it in the play:

> Fuck it, get the readers to become the storytellers. Call in with the news, their own lives, let them bring it to us rather than us chasing them [...] Isn't that the endpoint of the revolution? When they're producing their own content themselves? That's when we know they're really getting what they want.[202]

---

199 Jeremy Kareken, David Murrell and Gordon Farrell, *The Lifespan of a Fact*, unpublished script. I am grateful to Elaine Devlin Literary, Inc. and the Robert A. Freedman Dramatic Agency, Inc. for permission to reproduce these lines. I am also grateful to Jeremy Kareken for sharing the script with me.
200 James Graham, *Ink* (London: Bloomsbury, 2017), pp. 56–57.
201 Ibid., pp. 115.
202 Ibid., p. 44.

The playwright Lee Hall similarly emphasized how the modern media realm might become one that focused primarily on the generation of passionate opinion rather than on the relaying of fact. Hall created the play *Network* (National Theatre, London, 2017) based on Paddy Chayefsky's 1976 film of the same name, and the stage-drama revolves around an experienced TV news presenter, Howard Beale (played by Bryan Cranston) who has an on-air breakdown. Beale declares his intention to commit suicide, and therefore unwittingly creates a ratings hit. Ironically, viewers tune in, in increasing numbers, to watch the presenter's opinionated rants in which he denounces the media:

> Television is not the truth. Television is a goddam amusement park [...] We'll tell you any old shit you want to hear. None of it is true. Any idiot knows that. But you people sit there – all of you – day after day, night after night, all ages, colours, creeds, and this is all you know. You're beginning to believe this illusion we're spinning. You're beginning to think this is the true reality and it's your own lives that are unreal.[203]

The play may have been set in the 1970s, but in 2017 Hall argued that 'it's prophetic. It's about the birth of our current moment'.[204]

Our current moment, of course, is one in which a number of things have changed since the point when figures such as Sarah Kane were writing about journalists and the media. One central issue of our age is that many people now exist in news black spots, sometimes because local newspapers and local television reporting organizations have been hollowed out and closed down, and sometimes because malign political forces are operating against the perceived threat represented by the exchange of accurate information. As Margaret E. Roberts points out, today, authoritarian regimes such as that in China, 'have a large toolbox available to them to nudge citizens away from activist circles, dangerous information and focal points that could facilitate coordination'.[205] Yet, as social beings, people nonetheless still want to know what is going on outside of their immediate ken, and so gravitate towards places in the online world where stories of doubtful veracity can be circulated very quickly to millions of people. Readers may have no personal experience of the events encountered online, and those events may have nothing to do with the readers'

---

203 Lee Hall and Paddy Chayefsky, *Network* (London: Faber, 2017), p. 58.

204 Quoted by Sarah Hemming, 'I'm as mad as hell: Lee Hall on Bringing Network to the National Theatre', *Financial Times*, 20 October 2017, https://www.ft.com/content/f3655162-b32e-11e7-8007-554f9eaa90ba.

205 Margaret E. Roberts, *Censored: Distraction and Diversion inside China's Great Firewall* (Princeton: Princeton University Press, 2018), p. 11.

day-to-day lives. Indeed, those events may be grossly distorted or entirely fictive. But, nonetheless, as politicians and others have realized, audiences reading about such events can be encouraged and manipulated to feel a great cultural affinity with one side or another. We might feel deep love and gratitude towards certain figures and deep loathing towards others; we might feel deep emotion when confronted by fictional or fictionalized situations; and we might be moved by the deeds of vividly drawn heroes and villains. These concerns, in essence, are theatrical in nature, and constitute a modern analogue to concerns that have been central to staged drama since the time of Sophocles.

The mechanisms for news generation have obviously altered greatly in recent years. In 2019, for instance, *The New York Times* reported that a third of content published by Bloomberg News used some form of automated technology, with 'robot reporters' able to dissect financial reports in order to create immediate news articles.[206] Although the technology has changed, when we opt to access such online information, we become a kind of theatrical audience. Perhaps, then, we should not feel entirely surprised to realize that the issues we face when we stare into our laptops, tablets and mobile phones echo the concerns that have been experienced by playhouse audiences for many centuries.

Conclusion

Today, in the online twenty-first century, it is often difficult to distinguish between the illusory world of fabrication and the reality of lived experience, and commercially or politically savvy operators are able to exploit the blurring of those boundaries in order to disseminate ideas that have little basis in fact. As Harry G. Frankfurt put it in his influential book *On Bullshit* (1986, reprinted 2005), the essence of 'bullshit' can be found in 'just this lack of connection to a concern with truth – this indifference to how things really are'.[207] Yet that 'bullshit' is recognizable from earlier eras as well: it is the attitude that Ben Jonson's newsmongers endorse in *The Staple of News* when they sell news that is 'apocryphal [...] Or news of doubtful credit'.[208] It is the same attitude that David Hare and Howard Brenton's media mogul promotes in *Pravda*, when declaring: 'No one tells the truth. Why single out newspapers?'[209]

---

206 Cam Cottrill, 'The Rise of the Robot Reporter', *The New York Times*, 5 February 2019, https://www.nytimes.com/2019/02/05/business/media/artificial-intelligence-journalism-robots.html.

207 Harry G. Frankfurt, *On Bullshit* (Princeton: Princeton University Press, 2005), pp. 33–34.

208 Ben Jonson, p. 93.

209 Howard Brenton and David Hare, *Pravda* (rev. edn), pp. 103–4.

As I have emphasized in this book, theatre makers have repeatedly explored whether the news media might or might not report accurately on what has actually happened. In the first part of this volume we examined the performance aspect that is inherent in the genesis and realization of modern fake news, and in the second half we traced the long history of the Western theatre's engagement with the conceptual ideas surrounding fake news. Fake news is, as this book has noted, a tricky term, and may be manifested in different ways through different technologies and in different times and places, but some of the central concerns with which fake news is associated in our own time have a long history of being explored and analysed in the theatre. Today, as we live in the midst of an ever-more sophisticated and pervasive digital landscape and are often surrounded by the noise of populist politics, there is an increased urgency around questions about the fictive and real, about the role of artistic representation and about our own complicity in the dissemination of untruths. Indeed, the playwright Harold Pinter realized this towards the end of his life. In 1958, Pinter had asserted that 'There are no hard distinctions between what is real and what is unreal'. But he returned to, and revised, those words in his famous Nobel-prize-acceptance speech of 2005, insisting, 'As a citizen I must ask: What is true? What is false?' As Pinter concluded, 'to define the *real* truth of our lives and our societies is a crucial obligation which devolves upon us all'.[210]

---

210 Harold Pinter, 'Art, Truth & Politics', *The Nobel Prize in Literature 2005,* https:// www.nobelprize.org/prizes/literature/2005/pinter/25621-harold-pinter-nobel-lecture-2005/.

BIBLIOGRAPHY

Anderson, Benedict, *Imagined Communities*, rev. edn (London: Verso, 1991).

Arendt, Hannah, *The Human Condition*, 2nd edn (Chicago: University of Chicago Press, 1998).

Arent, Arthur, 'Ethiopia: The First "Living Newspaper"', *Education Theatre Journal*, 20:1 (1968), 15–31.

Augustine, *The Soliloquies of St Augustine*, trans. by Rose E. Cleveland (Boston: Little, Brown and Company, 1919).

Bairoch, Paul and Gary Goertz, 'Factors of Urbanisation in the Nineteenth Century Developed Countries', *Urban Studies*, 23:4 (1986), 285–305.

Balkin, Sarah, 'Rosmersholm', *Theatre Journal*, 63:3 (2011), 455–47.

Batey, Richard, *Jesus and the Forgotten City* (Grand Rapids: Baker, 1991).

Baumgartner, Jody C. and Jonathan S. Morris, *Laughing Matters: Humor and American Politics in the Media Age* (London: Routledge, 2008).

Beckett, Samuel, *Waiting for Godot* (London: Faber, 1965).

Benjamin, Walter, *Selected Writings: Volume 2, 1927–1934*, ed. by Michael W. Jennings, Howard Eiland, and Gary Smith, trans. by Rodney Livingston and others (Cambridge: Harvard University Press, 1999).

Bennett, Susan, *Theatre Audiences: A Theory of Production and Reception* (London: Routledge, 1997).

Bentley, Eric, *Thirty Years of Treason: Excerpts from Hearings before the House Committee on Un-American Activities, 1938–1968* (New York: Viking Press, 1971).

Berghaus, Günter, ed., 'Introduction', in *Fascism and Theatre: Comparative Studies on the Aesthetics and Politics of Performance in Europe, 1925–1945* (Providence: Berghahn, 1996), pp. 1–11.

Brake, Laurel, *Subjugated Knowledges: Journalism, Gender & Literature in the Nineteenth Century* (Houndmills: Macmillan, 1994).

Brecht, Bertolt, *Life of Galileo*, trans. by John Willett, ed. by John Willett and Ralph Manheim (London: Methuen, 2001).

Brecht, Bertolt, *The Resistible Rise of Arturo Ui*, in *Brecht: Collected Plays: Six*, trans. by Ralph Manheim and ed. by John Willett and Ralph Manheim (London: Methuen, 1994).

Brownlees, Nicholas, *The Language of Periodical News in Seventeenth-Century England* (Newcastle: Cambridge Scholars, 2011).

Bruner, Raisa, 'Donald Trump and Eminem Weren't Always Enemies. Here's Proof', *Time*, 11 October 2017. https://time.com/4978126/trump-eminem-endorsement/.

Casson, John W., 'Living Newspaper: Theatre and Therapy', *The Drama Review*, 44:2 (2000), 107–22.

Cavallo, Pietro, 'Theatre Politics of the Mussolini Régime and Their Influence on Fascist Drama', in *Fascism and Theatre: Comparative Studies on the Aesthetics and Politics of Performance in Europe, 1925–1945*, ed. by Günter Berghaus (Providence: Berghahn, 1996), pp. 113–32.

Cobb, Gerry, '"Injunction Granted" in Its Times: A Living Newspaper Reappraised', *New Theatre Quarterly*, 6:23 (1990), 279–96.

Cottrill, Cam, 'The Rise of the Robot Reporter', *The New York Times*, 5 February 2019. https://www.nytimes.com/2019/02/05/business/media/artificial-intelligence-journalism-robots.html.

Cox, Jordanna, 'The Phantom Public, the Living Newspaper: Reanimating the Public in the Federal Theatre Project's 1935 (New York, 1935)', *Theatre Survey*, 58:3 (September 2017), 300–25.

Curtis, Adam, *Bitter Lake*, Prod. Lucy Kelsall, BBC, 25 January 2015.

Diderot, Denis, *The Paradox of Acting*, trans. by Walter Herries Pollock (New York: Hill & Wang, 1957).

Dolzhansky, Roman, 'Lyrical Heroism', *Kommersant*, 17 January 2011. http://www.smotr.ru/2010/2010_tab_0.htm.

Donaldson, Ian, *Ben Jonson: A Life* (Oxford: Oxford University Press, 2011).

'Donald Trump Bodyslams, Beats and Shaves Vince McMahon at Wrestlemania XXIII'. https://www.youtube.com/watch?v=MMKFIHRpe71.

Drain, Richard, *Twentieth-Century Theatre: A Sourcebook* (London: Routledge, 1995).

Dubovitsky, Natan and Vladislav Surkov, *Almost Zero*, trans. by Nino Gojiashvili and Nastya Valentine (RareAudioBooks.com).

Edemariam, Aida, 'The Cost of Survival', *The Guardian*, 5 May 2004. https://www.theguardian.com/world/2004/mar/05/southafrica.books.

Everyman, in *The Norton Anthology of English Literature: Eighth Edition: Volume A: The Middle Ages*, ed. by Alfred David and James Simpson (New York: W. W. Norton & Company, 2006), pp. 463–84.

Farhi, Paul, 'Trump's First News Conference since Election Blasts a Usual Suspect: The Media', *The Washington Post*, 11 January 2017. https://www.washingtonpost.com/lifestyle/style/trumps-first-news-conference-since-election-blasts-a-usual-suspect-the-media/2017/01/11/e1d2e84c-d823-11e6-9a36-1d296534b31e_story.html.

Finglass, P.J., 'Commentary', in Sophocles, *Oedipus the King*, ed. and trans. by P.J. Finglass (Cambridge: Cambridge University Press, 2018), pp. 163–619.

Flanagan, Hallie, *Arena: The History of the Federal Theatre* (New York: Benjamin Blom, 1940).

Flood, Alison, 'Fake News Is "Very Real" Word of the Year for 2017', *The Guardian*, 2 November 2017. https://www.theguardian.com/books/2017/nov/02/fake-news-is-very-real-word-of-the-year-for-2017.

Foer, Franklin, 'The Era of Fake Video Begins', *The Atlantic*, May 2018. https://www.theatlantic.com/magazine/archive/2018/05/realitys-end/556877/.

Foster, Roy, *W.B. Yeats: A Life: 1: The Apprentice Mage* (Oxford: Oxford University Press, 1998).

Foy, Henry, 'Vladislav Surkov: "An Overdose of Freedom Is Lethal to a State', *Financial Times*, 18 June 2021. https://www.ft.com/content/1324acbb-f475-47ab-a914-4a96a9d14bac.

Frankfurt, Harry G., *On Bullshit* (Princeton: Princeton University Press, 2005).

Gelfert, Alex, 'Fake News: A Definition', *Informal Logic*, 38:1 (2018), 84–117.

Gottesman, Alex, *Politics and the Street in Democratic Athens* (Cambridge: Cambridge University Press, 2014).

Graham-Harrison, Emma, '"Enemy of the People": Trump's Phrase and Its Echoes of Totalitarianism', *The Guardian*, 3 August 2018. https://www.theguardian.com/us-news/2018/aug/03/trump-enemy-of-the-people-meaning-history.

Graham, James, *Ink* (London: Bloomsbury, 2017).

Habermas, Jürgen, *The Structural Transformation of the Public Sphere*, trans. by Thomas Burger (Cambridge: Polity Press, 1992).

Haddow, Sam, 'A Rebellious Past: History, Theatre and the England Riots', *Studies in Theatre and Performance*, 35:1 (2015), 7–21.

Hahl, Oliver, Minjae Kim and Ezra W. Zuckerman, 'The Authentic Appeal of the Lying Demagogue: Proclaiming the Deeper Truth about Political Illegitimacy', *American Sociological Review*, 83:1 (2018), 1–33.

Hall, Lee, and Paddy Chayefsky, *Network* (London: Faber, 2017).

Hansberry, Lorraine, *Les Blancs*, final text adapted by Robert Nimiroff (London: Samuel French, 1972).

Hare, David, 'David Hare & Max Stafford-Clark', *Verbatim Verbatim: Contemporary Documentary Theatre*, ed. by Will Hammond and Dan Steward (London: Oberon, 2008), pp. 45–76.

Hare, David, *Obedience, Struggle & Revolt* (London: Faber, 2005).

Hare, David, and Howard Brenton, *Pravda* (London: Methuen, 1985).

Hare, David, and Howard Brenton, *Pravda*, rev. edn (London: Bloomsbury, 2015 [1986]).

Harker, Ben, 'Mediating the 1930s: Documentary and Politics in Theatre Union's *Last Edition* (1940)', in *Get Real: Documentary Theatre Past and Present*, ed. by Alison Forsyth and Chris Megson (Houndmills: Palgrave, 2009), pp. 24–37.

Harp, Richard, 'Jonson's Late Plays', in *The Cambridge Companion to Ben Jonson*, ed. by Richard Harp and Stanley Stewart (Cambridge: Cambridge University Press, 2000), pp. 90–102.

Hecht, Ben, and Charles MacArthur, *The Front Page* (New York: Samuel French, 1950).

Hemming, Sarah, 'I'm as mad as Hell: Lee Hall on Bringing Network to the National Theatre', *Financial Times*, 20 October 2017. https://www.ft.com/content/f3655162-b32e-11e7-8007-554f9eaa90ba.

Holroyd, Michael, *Bernard Shaw: The One-Volume Definitive Edition* (London: Vintage, 1998).

Ibsen, Henrik, *An Enemy of the People*, in Ibsen, *Ibsen: Volume VI*, trans. and ed. by James Walter McFarlane (Oxford: Oxford University Press, 1960), pp. 19–126.

Ibsen, Henrik, *Rosmersholm*, in Ibsen, *Ibsen: Volume VI*, trans. and ed. by James Walter McFarlane (Oxford: Oxford University Press, 1960), pp. 289–422.

Irwin, Elizabeth, *Solon and Early Greek Poetry: The Politics of Exhortation* (Cambridge: Cambridge University Press, 2005).

Jonson, Ben, *The Staple of News*, ed. by Anthony Parr (Manchester: Manchester University Press, 1988).

Kane, Paul, 'Hillary Clinton Attacks "Fake News" in Post-Election Appearance on Capitol Hill', *The Washington Post*, 9 December 2016. https://www.washingtonpost.com/news/powerpost/wp/2016/12/08/hillary-clinton-attacks-fake-news-in-post-election-appearance-on-capitol-hill/.

Kane, Sarah, *Complete Plays* (London: Methuen, 2001).

Kang, Jaeho, 'The *Ur*-History of Media Space: Walter Benjamin and the Information Industry in Nineteenth-Century Paris', *International Journal of Politics, Culture, and Society*, 22:2 (2009), 231–48.

Kareken, Jeremy, David Murrell, and Gordon Farrell, *The Lifespan of a Fact*, unpublished script.

Kelly, Meg, 'President Trump Cries "Fake News" and the World Follows', *The Washington Post*, 6 February 2018. https://www.washingtonpost.com/news/fact-checker/wp/2018/02/06/president-trump-cries-fake-news-and-the-world-follows/?utm_term=.31e629caf8f4.

Kent, Nicolas, 'Nicolas Kent', in *Verbatim Verbatim: Contemporary Documentary Theatre*, ed. by Will Hammond and Dan Steward (London: Oberon, 2008), pp. 133–68.

Kershner, James W., *The Elements of News Writing* (Boston: Allyn & Bacon, 2005).

Kirkwood, Lucy, *Chimerica* (London: Nick Hern, 2013).

Kirkwood, Lucy, *Chimerica*, episode 1, Channel 4, 17 April 2019.

Kovach, Bill and Tom Rosenstiel, *The Elements of Journalism*, rev. edn (New York: Three Rivers Press, 2007).

Le Bon, Gustave, *The Crowd* (New Brunswick: Transaction Publishers, 1995).

Leach, Robert, *Revolutionary Theatre* (London: Routledge, 1994).

Leary, Alex, 'Trump: "And I Was in Florida with 25,000 People Going Wild', *Tampa Bay Times*, 21 March 2018. https://www.tampabay.com/florida-politics/buzz/2018/03/20/and-i-was-in-florida-with-25000-people-going-wild/.

Linklater, Magnus, 'Slog Times, All the Time' *Observer*, 29 December 1991, p. 43.

Littlewood, Joan, and Jimmy Miller, *Last Edition*, Ruskin College Oxford, Ewan MacColl and Peggy Seeger Archive.

Lonsdale, Sarah, *The Journalist in British Fiction and Film* (London: Bloomsbury, 2016).

'"Lügenpresse" ist Unwort des Jahres', *Spiegel*, 13 January 2015. http://www.spiegel.de/kultur/gesellschaft/luegenpresse-ist-unwort-des-jahres-a-1012678.html.

Mathews, Jane DeHart, *Federal Theatre, 1935–1939: Plays, Relief, and Politics* (Princeton: Princeton University Press, 1967).

McDermott, Emmet, 'Donald Trump Campaign Offered Actors $50 to Cheer for Him at Presidential Announcement', *Hollywood Reporter*, 17 June 2015. https://www.hollywoodreporter.com/news/donald-trump-campaign-offered-actors-803161.

Meek, James, 'The Club and the Mob', *London Review of Books*, 6 December 2018, pp. 9–16.

Munday, Anthony, 'A Second and Third Blast of Retreat from Plays and Theaters', in *Shakespeare's Theatre: A Sourcebook*, ed. by Tanya Pollard (Oxford: Blackwell, 2004), pp. 62–83.

Nicas, Jack, 'Alex Jones Said Bans Would Strengthen Him. He Was Wrong', *The New York Times*, 4 September 2018. https://www.nytimes.com/2018/09/04/technology/alex-jones-infowards-bans-traffic.html.

Norton-Taylor, Richard, 'MI5 Surveillance of Joan Littlewood During War Led to Two-Year BBC Ban', *The Guardian*, 4 March 2008. https://www.theguardian.com/world/2008/mar/04/secondworldwar.past.

Norton-Taylor, Richard, 'Richard Norton-Taylor', in *Verbatim Verbatim: Contemporary Documentary Theatre*, ed. by Will Hammond and Dan Steward (London: Oberon, 2008), pp. 103–32.

O'Connor, John S., '*Spirochette* and the War on Syphilis', *The Drama Review*, 21:1 (1977), 91–98.

O'Mahony, John, 'Piques and Troughs', *The Guardian*, 25 May 2002. https://www.theguardian.com/books/2002/may/25/arts.artsfeatures.

'Oxford Dictionaries Word of the Year 2016 Is...', 16 November 2016. https://www.oxforddictionaries.com/press/news/2016/12/11/WOTY-16.

Pinkard, Terry, *Hegel: A Biography* (Cambridge: Cambridge University Press, 2000).

Pinter, Harold, 'Art, Truth & Politics', *The Nobel Prize in Literature 2005*. https://www.nobelprize.org/prizes/literature/2005/pinter/25621-harold-pinter-nobel-lecture-2005/.

Plato, *Republic: Books 6–10*, ed. by Chris Emlyn-Jones and William Preddy (Cambridge, MA: Harvard University Press, 2013).

'Playwright Gillian Slovo Talks about England Riots Play', *Front Row*, BBC Radio 4, 23 November 2011. http://www.bbc.co.uk/news/entertainment-arts-15856868.

Pomerantsev, Peter, *Nothing Is True and Everything Is Possible* (London: Faber, 2015).

Pomerantsev, Peter, 'The Hidden Author of Putinism', *The Atlantic*, 7 November 2014. https://www.theatlantic.com/international/archive/2014/11/hidden-author-putinism-russia-vladislav-surkov/382489/.

Poulain, Alexandra, *Irish Drama, Modernity and the Passion Play* (London: Palgrave Macmillan, 2016).

Pound, Ezra, *Plays Modelled on the Noh*, ed. by Donald C. Gallup (Toledo: The Friends of the University of Toledo Libraries, 1987).

Reinelt, Janelle, 'Towards a Poetics of Theatre and Public Events', *The Drama Review*, 50:3 (2006), 69–87.

Richardson, Kay, Katy Parry, and John Corner, *Political Culture and Media Genre: Beyond the News* (Houndmills: Palgrave Macmillan, 2013).

Rickard, Jane, 'A Divided Jonson?: Art and Truth in "The Staple of News"', *English Literary Renaissance*, 42:2 (2012), 294–316.

Rini, Regina, 'Fake News and Partisan Epistemology', *Kennedy Institute of Ethics Journal*. https://kiej.georgetown.edu/category/uncategorized/special-issue/special-issue-trump-and-the-2016-election/.

Roberts, Margaret E., *Censored: Distraction and Diversion inside China's Great Firewall* (Princeton: Princeton University Press, 2018).

Robinson, Joanna, 'The Performance of Anti-Theatrical Prejudice in a Provincial Victorian Town: Nottingham and Its New Theatre Royal, 1865', *Nineteenth Century Theatre and Film*, 35:2 (2008), 10–28.

Schudson, Michael, *The Sociology of News* (New York: W. W. Norton & Company, 2003).

Shakespeare, William, *The New Oxford Shakespeare: The Complete Works, Modern Critical Edition*, ed. by Gary Taylor, John Jowett, Terri Bourus, and Gabriel Egan (Oxford: Oxford University Press, 2016).

Shaw, Bernard, *O'Flaherty, V.C.* in George Bernard Shaw, *Playlets*, ed. by James Moran (Oxford: Oxford University Press, 2021), pp. 145–70.

Soans, Robin, 'Robin Soans', in *Verbatim Verbatim: Contemporary Documentary Theatre*, ed. by Will Hammond and Dan Steward (London: Oberon, 2008), pp. 15–44.

Spencer, Albert R., 'The Dialogues as Dramatic Rehearsal: Plato's Republic and the Moral Accounting Metaphor', *The Pluralist*, 8:2 (2013), 26–35.

Stafford-Clark, Max, 'David Hare & Max Stafford-Clark', *Verbatim Verbatim: Contemporary Documentary Theatre*, ed. by Will Hammond and Dan Steward (London: Oberon, 2008), pp. 45–76.

Stanislavski, Constantin, *An Actor Prepares*, trans. by Elizabeth Reynolds Hapgood (London: Bloomsbury, 2013).

Stoppard, Tom, 'My Love Affair with Newspapers', *British Journalism Review*, 16:4 (2005), 19–29.

Stoppard, Tom, *Tom Stoppard Plays 5* (London: Faber, 1999), pp. 247–359.

Suskind, Ron, 'Faith, Certainty and the Presidency of George W. Bush', *The New York Times*, 17 October 2004. https://www.nytimes.com/2004/10/17/magazine/faith-certainty-and-the-presidency-of-george-w-bush.html.

Tandoc Jr., Edson C., Zheng Wei Lim, and Richard Ling, 'Defining "Fake News"', *Digital Journalism*, 6:2 (2018), 137–53.

The Digital, Culture, Media and Sport Committee, 'Disinformation and "Fake News": Interim Report' 29 July 2018. https://publications.parliament.uk/pa/cm201719/cmselect/cmcumeds/363/363.pdf.

'The Play: The Living Newspaper Finally Gets Under Way', *The New York Times*, 16 March 1936.

Theatre Workshop, *Oh What a Lovely War* (London: Methuen, 1992).

Thompson, Doug, 'The Organisation, Fascistisation and Management of Theatre in Italy, 1925–1943', in *Fascism and Theatre: Comparative Studies on the Aesthetics and Politics of Performance in Europe, 1925–1945*, ed. by Günter Berghaus (Providence: Berghahn, 1995), pp. 94–112.

Timberg, Craig, Karla Adam, and Michael Kranish, 'Bannon Oversaw Cambridge Analytica's Collection of Facebook Data, According to Former Employee', *The Washington Post*, 20 March 2018. https://www.washingtonpost.com/politics/bannon-oversaw-cambridge-analyticas-collection-of-facebook-data-according-to-former-employee/2018/03/20/8fb369a6-2c55-11e8-b0b0-f706877db618_story.html?utm_term=.01dc0d5fa6ff.

Trump, Donald, 'Remarks by President Trump at the Veterans of Foreign Wars of the United States National Convention', Kansas City, 24 July 2018. https://www.whitehouse.gov/briefings-statements/remarks-president-trump-veterans-foreign-wars-united-states-national-convention-kansas-city-mo/.

Trump, Donald, Twitter message of 9 October 2018. https://twitter.com/realdonaldtrump/status/1049638803177127936?lang=en.

Wardle, Claire, 'Fake News. It's Complicated', *First Draft*, 16 February 2017. https://firstdraftnews.org/fake-news-complicated/.

Wendling, Mike, 'BBC Trending: The (Almost) Complete History of 'Fake News', 22 January 2018. https://www.bbc.co.uk/news/blogs-trending-42724320.

Wesker, Arnold, *Journey into Journalism* (London: Writers and Readers Publishing Cooperative, 1977).

Wesker, Arnold, *The Journalists, The Wedding Feast, Shylock* (London: Penguin, 1990).

Wilde, Oscar, 'The Decay of Lying: An Observation', in *The Complete Works of Oscar Wilde: Volume 4: Criticism: Historical Criticism, Intentions, The Soul of Man*, ed. by Josephine M. Guy (Oxford: Oxford University Press, 2007), pp. 73–103.

Williams, Bernard, *Truth and Truthfulness* (Princeton: Princeton University Press, 2002).

Williams, Raymond, *Drama in a Dramatised Society: An Inaugural Lecture* (Cambridge: Cambridge University Press, 1975).

Williams, Raymond, 'Theatre as a Political Forum', in *The Politics of Modernism: Against the New Conformists*, ed. by Tony Pinkney (London: Verso, 1989).

Williamson, Elizabeth, 'Truth in a Post-Truth Era: Sandy Hook Families Sue Alex Jones, Conspiracy Theorist', *The New York Times*, 23 May 2018. https://www.nytimes.com/2018/05/23/us/politics/alex-jones-trump-sandy-hook.html.

Worley, Will, 'InfoWars' Alex Jones Is a 'Performance Artist Playing a Character', Says His Lawyer', *Independent*, 17 April 2017. https://www.independent.co.uk/news/infowards-alex-jones-performance-artist-playing-character-lawyer-conspiracy-theory-donald-trump-a7687571.html.

Zimdars, Melissa, 'Introduction', in *Fake News: Understanding Media and Misinformation in the Digital Age*, ed. by Melissa Zimdars and Kembrew McLeod (Cambridge: MIT Press, 2020), pp. 13–18.

Žižek, Slavoj, 'Three Variations on Trump: Chaos, Europe, and Fake News', *The Philosophical Salon*. https://thephilosophicalsalon.com/three-variations-on-trump-chaos-europe-and-fake-news/.

INDEX

Printed in the USA
CPSIA information can be obtained
at www.ICGtesting.com
JSHW021315110324
58992JS00004B/115